Oct 18/2016

Mired Best Wishi
Herb !

GRAB THE
WHEEL
AND GO!

Planning Your Journey Through Life

Herb Singer

with John Lawrence Reynolds

 FriesenPress

Suite 300 - 990 Fort St
Victoria, BC, V8V 3K2
Canada

www.friesenpress.com

ISBN
978-1-4602-7573-3 (Hardcover)
978-1-4602-7572-6 (Paperback)
978-1-4602-7574-0 (eBook)

1. BIOGRAPHY & AUTOBIOGRAPHY, BUSINESS

Distributed to the trade by The Ingram Book Company

TABLE OF CONTENTS

ACKNOWLEDGEMENTS

I intended this book to be a lesson for those who cared to learn from my life experience. Telling my own story, however, took a lot of assistance from other people, and I need to express my thanks to them.

Without the support of my wife Rhoda through the years I could never have accomplished all the achievements in this book. I must also recognize the role of our kids Barry, Jay and Sarah. Thanks for behaving nicely, growing up without giving us any headaches, and helping build our business for your future.

I want to thank all of our staff who worked hard over the years to aid in our success. Thanks also to our licensees, especially Tino Carrara who bought into the vision and grew with it.

Last but not least thanks to John Lawrence Reynolds, who helped tell our story and spent many hours discussing the contents with me. He really got involved in the tale, and learned to appreciate good pastrami along the way.

ONE

We All Need a Road Map Through Life

When it comes to pondering their journey through life, too many people act like they're Christopher Columbus.

"Is that such a bad thing?" I hear you ask. "After all, the guy got the King of Spain to cover his expenses, which involved buying him three ships to make the trip across the ocean. He found America, brought back tons of gold and trinkets, became one of the most famous people in the world, had a city in Ohio named after him, and retired in comfort. What's so bad about that?"

Okay, he was lucky. He was also wrong. He wasn't looking for America (which had already been "found" by all the indigenous people living there).

I should remind you that he set out looking for India, which he missed by 16,000 kilometres, give or take a few. For this he's a hero? Nobody thinks of the other guys who set sail to find glory and fortune with the same kind of planning that Columbus made, namely none. When they vanished, everyone assumed they fell off the edge of the flat earth. Obviously, they didn't do much planning.

Columbus couldn't plan much beyond "sail west and stay calm". But when it comes to thinking about the rest of *your* life, you have choices to make. Unlike Columbus, you can make a plan and follow through on it. I'll go even further: When it comes to making plans for your life, you have an obligation to yourself and to all of those around you, especially your family. If your only plan is to stumble down a darkened road with no idea where you are going and, what's worse, not caring, you are likely to end up feeling very unfulfilled. Unfulfilled people do not tend to be happy and are not much fun to be around. People who have an idea about who they are and what they want to do with their lives are more satisfied with themselves — even if they don't reach their goal. It's the *trying* that's important.

Look at it this way:

Few of us will ever reach the pinnacle of whatever we aim for in life. There can only be one President of the United States, one Prime Minister of Canada, one Oscar winner for Best Actor, and one Nobel Prize Peace Prize winner at any one time. If we don't reach the top of whatever category we choose to live our lives within, it's a disappointment. But it's not a tragedy.

You want a tragedy? Here's a tragedy: Having a dream and never trying to make it come true. Here's another one: Refusing to plan any further in life than the next paycheque, the next Saturday night party, or your next birthday, then looking around when you're sixty years old and saying, "This trip is nearly over, and I didn't get anywhere I wanted to go!"

My Dream

My dream was to become a millionaire.

"Boy, that sounds materialistic!" I hear somebody saying. Well, it was and it wasn't.

Here's why: My dream didn't just involve dollars in the bank.

I wanted to have a lifelong partnership with a woman whose abilities complemented my own, a person who shared the same dream with me. I wanted a family that would do me proud and, in turn, would be proud of me. I wanted to build something that involved gifted people who enjoyed their work and who I could compensate for all the support they provided me and the organization that I created. And I wanted, at some point in my life, to look back at what I had achieved, nod my head, and say, "Not bad, Herb. Not bad at all."

I think I'm there.

One more thing.

I wanted at some point to share my experience and the wisdom I was to accumulate with other people. This is why I wrote this book. So I'm glad you're here to read it.

I promise not to preach, and I'll try not to boast. I'll even try to make you smile from time to time. Maybe you'll find yourself nodding your head in understanding.

The last thing I want to do on these pages is bore you. And I probably won't because my life has been anything but boring.

Life Is a Journey

You've heard that line before. You may have heard it so often that it sounds like a cliché to you. But here's something to think about: A cliché is a cliché because it is true.

In many ways, we all start out in the same place, and we all end up in the same place. We are all born, and we all die. It's what we do in the space between those years that counts.

The biggest difference between you and me is the journey we take. It's called "life". It'll be a long trip, if you're lucky. How long? Well, if you're a young person anticipating the journey, you could have fifty or more years of travel ahead of you.

But no matter what truck stop you find yourself at along the way, you should ask yourself the same questions you would ask if you were planning any long journey for business or for pleasure. (In my case, it was both.)

You should ask: Where do I want to go? How will I get there? How will I pay for it? Who would I like to travel with? What do I plan to see along the way? What kinds of things do I want to avoid? How often do I want to stop for a while and look around? What kinds of souvenirs would I like to collect?

Many people pay no attention to the first question, and ultimately, they don't give much thought to the others. Or they think they have the answer to the first question, so the others will sort themselves out. But it doesn't work that way. Here's the cold hard fact: Nobody has answers to any of these questions at the beginning. Only later. Much later. But you still have to ask them because they are too important to ignore.

Deciding on what you want to be. Wondering how to get there.

Young people who have given even the smallest amount of thought to their journey through life may say, "I want to be a doctor," or "I want to be an actor," or "I want to work with underprivileged children and make the world a better place."

By defining what they want to become, they believe they have settled on how they want to get there.

"I'll go to medical school, do an internship, start a practice, go to conferences, and maybe play some golf," the wannabe doctor might say.

"I'll go to drama school, wait on tables to pay my way, and get life experience, and I'll never turn down an audition," I hear the actor saying.

"I'll work on getting a degree in social work, look for some inner-city assignments, and maybe learn to play guitar, and sing folk songs," the worker with underprivileged kids could suggest. Well, good for them. But they're missing the point.

Just because you know where you're headed doesn't mean you've mapped out your journey.

Knowing where you're going may make reaching your goal a little clearer, but that's just the beginning. All kinds of things can go badly. Maybe you're on the wrong road or headed in the wrong direction. Maybe you are not aware that the road you've chosen leads to a dead end. Or maybe you're not prepared for potholes, detours, steep hills, and sharp curves.

That's why you need to plan for your journey — and to do that, you need a map.

And guess what?

God didn't give you one.

Finding the Map

"How do I plot a journey without a road map?" I hear you asking. (I'm showing my age. These days you're probably looking for a GPS.) Whatever it is, you need one. Here's why: Some people prefer to be happy wanderers, going through life hoping to be surprised at how everything turns out.

"Who knows where I'll end up?" the happy wanderer says.

It's true. When you first set out, you don't know where your travels will take you along your journey.

You could be lucky, stumble into a bed of roses, and remain there, content to roll around happily, just letting things happen to you. Or you could be easily satisfied, floating like a bubble on the breeze.

Just remember what eventually happens to bubbles.

You could also win a lottery and be worry-free, financially speaking, for the rest of your life.

Just remember this: The odds of picking that winning 649 Llottery ticket are about 14,000,000 to one. Count all the zeroes. And check out all the sad stories from the lottery winners who failed to find either long-lasting happiness or satisfaction after winning enormous sums of money they hadn't really earned.

You can leave things to chance, or you can draw your own map. Neither choice guarantees success, but if you're searching for guarantees, life is the wrong place to look. Rely on a map. At least you'll be more in control of things.

The way I see it, you need four things to create a map for your life's journey, and they don't include pens, paper, or computer programs. The four tools you need are all within your own mind.

Here's what they are and why you need them.

AMBITION

If you have ambition, you want to be a little more satisfied the next year than the year before. It's not about having an all-encompassing hunger that eats away at you inside. It has nothing to do with having a house, or a car, or income, or status. It isn't about what you think you deserve or your sacrifices. It's about satisfying a need that is deeply within you.

For most people, ambition is so deeply ingrained that they aren't even aware they have it.

I happen to believe that every person who gets up in the morning and heads off to put in a day's work at a full-time job has ambition.

It's important to use your ambition to define your goals and set a course for the places you want to travel throughout your life. Let's suppose your ambition is to become a teacher. You can call yourself a teacher after completing all the education and passing all the tests needed. You can probably achieve this goal by your mid-twenties. But it doesn't really mean much. That's because the next step — the true destination of your journey — should be to become the *best teacher* possible — *The World's Champion of Dedicated and Acclaimed Teachers, Whose Prowess and Competence Are Praised by Students Everywhere!*

Or something like that.

Will you get there? Doesn't matter. The important thing is to have a goal and try to reach it.

IDENTITY

Having identity means you are honest with yourself about who you are, regardless of what others may think of you or say about you.

Identity is not about seeking fame and envying your neighbour because he got his name in the news (in a good way), and you didn't. It's about accepting who and what you are and moving on from there. Much of a person's identity comes from things they can't control, like their place of origin, their DNA, or their social status.

You can be born into a wealthy family with great social standing and all the comforts you could ever want, but that doesn't guarantee anything. Let's face it: If you're on top of the mountain, about the only place you can go is down.

Maybe you were raised in poverty, with no shoes on your feet, no food in the refrigerator — maybe even no refrigerator –and with no one to give you a hand up. If so, congratulations! No, really.

If you are born with a need to survive, somewhere within you is the power you need to accept responsibility for your own actions, plan for your own happiness, grow determined to succeed, and relish every measure of your success because you did it on your own, and you don't owe anyone else a thing. I'm not being ironic here. I really mean it. Some of the greatest achievements in history were made by people like me who began with nothing. If this is you, your destination won't be just a goal. It will be your identity. I speak with authority because I came from that kind of background.

No shoes and no food?

Now I have lots of shoes to put on my feet. And I eat very well.

Like I said earlier, none of us has a choice about where we arrive in this world or about our circumstances. We can cry, complain, or get really angry about it, which I can promise you, won't make a dime's worth of difference. Or we can abide by this brilliant observation:

What you've got is what you've got.
What you do with it is who you are.

VISION

You have vision if you are able to close your eyes and see yourself having achieved various goals. I think of vision as a combination of daydreaming and planning. You picture yourself at the highest point in your journey and imagine the enjoyment you'll get from it. You freeze that picture in your mind. Then you use it as inspiration to keep moving past all the challenges of life. That's how it works.

It's your vision and your journey. It's no one else's. So don't let anyone suggest that you are aiming too high or that your dreams are unrealistic. Nothing within the scope of human ability is impossible to achieve if you want it badly enough, and striving to achieve it — even if you fail — is far better than never having tried.

My vision through my childhood and young adult years was to become as wealthy as I could without doing something immoral or illegal. I never ignored that vision. I was like a horse wearing blinders who was able to see only the vision ahead of it on the far horizon, just over the next hill — and the one after that.

Once you have your vision fixed in your mind, you need to develop an attitude that says, in effect, "I am on a journey carrying me toward my vision. Nobody else has taken this exact route in the past because I am unique like everyone else in the world. Nobody else will be taking the same journey in the future because too many things will have changed. And if I keep the right attitude, stay with my plan, and listen to the advice from people who have learned something from their own journey, I can make my vision a reality."

We never know just what we are capable of achieving until we are faced with circumstances and our own determination.

Want proof?

Imagine running a marathon. That's 40 kilometres or 26 miles, if you prefer. For most of us, it's tough even to think of doing such a thing. Now imagine running a marathon every day. You get up in the morning, you run 40 kilometres up and down hills in cold rain and baking sunshine. You go to sleep that night, and the next day you do the same thing, over and over.

"Whoa," you say. "That's a little too much to ask."

I'm not finished.

Now imagine running a full marathon every day on one leg. Most of you know where I am going.

Terry Fox did that when he was 21 years old. He ran a marathon a day with a prosthesis replacing the right leg he had lost to cancer, for 143 days, covering 5,373 kilometres or 3,339 miles. He planned to continue running all across Canada, but the return of cancer cut his efforts short. He died the following year.

Terry Fox's experience was both a tragedy and an inspiration. Dying from cancer at age 22 is a tragedy no matter how you measure it. But his life is also an inspiration to anyone whose goal may be considered too bold, or too pie-in-the-sky to consider. I don't know if Terry Fox would have preferred to have spent his last year of life reclining in his family's back yard rather than drawing attention to the need for cancer research by running a marathon a day. But if he had been aware that cancer would strike him down in the same way, and at the same time, whether he did his run or not, I suspect he would have chosen to do the run. During his run he raised $1.7 million for cancer research. A year later, at his death, he had raised $23 million. Since then, events inspired by Terry Fox have raised an estimated $100 million or more, all of it aimed at finding a way to prevent cancer from claiming lives — especially the lives of people like him.

Terry Fox needed a goal to aim for, and in one small way or another, each of us is better for the fact that he tried.

Remember my line:

What you've got is what you've got.

What you do with it is who you are.

My maxim could have been written with Terry Fox in mind. Look what he was handed by life. Look what he did with it. And look who he became.

Sometimes, I think the saddest people in the world are the ones lying on their deathbeds, recalling the visions of things they wanted to do with their lives and the ambitions they once had but ignored. They are saying to themselves, "I never even tried…" That's so sad.

PRIDE

If you have pride, it doesn't mean you are arrogant or have a big ego. It just means that you stand for some things and deserve recognition or reward for your effort. Pride is like the password you use to access your bank account. You know you need it, and you use it when you have to, but you tend not to show it to anybody. Unfortunately, too many people think pride is like a trumpet, an instrument for blaring their own sense of personal status or accomplishment to the world. The dictionary defines this as "hubris".

Hubris is not my choice for a definition of pride and definitely not my style. I think of pride as satisfaction with, and attachment to, your own personal choices, values, and actions.

That sounds a little stuffy and textbookish, doesn't it?

Okay, how about this:

Pride is like underwear.

We all need to wear it.

We just don't need to show it.

If you can develop and harness these four elements, you're at least as well equipped as Columbus when it comes to working out plans for a life's journey. And you won't have to worry about falling off the edge of the earth or getting scurvy, for that matter.

See? Things could be worse.

Most of the happy and successful people I have dealt with over my years have all *four* qualities to one degree or another.

Which finally brings us to me — my road map (or GPS), my journey, my lessons, and my advice.

Why Listen to Herb?

Let's begin with me asking the obvious question and providing the best answer I can come up with. The question: "Why should I listen to Herb Singer's advice about planning for life?" Followed by: "We're all individuals. Who says I'm supposed to follow in his footsteps?"

I don't want you to follow in my footsteps. Don't even try. You need to hold onto your unique identity and take pride in it, which is hard to do if you're trying to be like someone else — namely me. Of the 7 billion people in the world, nobody else is exactly like you. I don't want you to follow in my footsteps; I just want you to follow my advice.

Why?

I have covered more ground in my journey than you have in life — unless you are older than me. I have gone on ahead, as it were, and bumped along the ruts, driven down the dead-end roads, and come upon some of the same scenery you are likely to encounter. We won't have seen all of the same places on our unique journeys, but I'm sure we'll have encountered some of the same ruts.

The truth is, I don't want this book to be about Herb Singer. I want it to be about *you*. I want you to be aware that you're not on an out-of-control roller coaster ride going up one hill, down another, twisting and turning your way back to earth again. And you're not alone out there with nothing to do but hold on, trying not to scream.

If you are, you shouldn't be.

Don't get me wrong. It's your journey, your carnival ride, so you should decide, as much as possible, where the ride goes.

I just want to warn you: Life is better if you avoid the rides that make you scream.

At some point, on every carnival ride, you realize that the ride is almost over, and you are coming back down to earth. In life, it happens chemically. Something in your body changes, and one morning you wake up to a telephone call from God. (He's not much for handing out road maps, but he's pretty good at phoning and waking you up when you need it.)

My Epiphany

My wake-up call arrived when I turned 60 years old. To some people, the call arrives at 55. Others get the message at 65 or 70. But it always arrives. And it's always a shocker.

By that time, I had achieved most of the goals I had set for myself as a kid growing up in Brooklyn. My wake-up call at 60 was to tell me that I had, if I was lucky, about 20 more years before my ride was over. Maybe a little more, maybe a little less, but 20 years was about all I figure anyone at my age could count on.

The thought wasn't totally depressing. I could hardly believe I was singled out not to live forever. That's one thing I have in common with every other unique individual on earth.

It made me think, however, of what I wanted to do with those twenty years or so left to me. How would I feel if I was facing just twenty years more of life and hadn't accomplished the things I had wanted to achieve? Or what if I hadn't given the whole journey much thought at all, and just drifted along, lost in the forest instead of being out on the road? What would I have? I'll tell you what I would have — a ton of regrets.

Regrets are not things you want to have hanging around when you're in your 60s. So I decided I would go over my life, identify the way I had planned things to happen, examine how I handled the things I *hadn't* planned to happen, and look for lessons that others could use on their own journeys.

All the mistakes, missteps, and achievements are in this book.

One more thing about this journey of ours.

If mine were taken in a car (rented from Discount, but never mind), I could say that, despite all the challenges and all the detours, washed-out bridges, heavy traffic, and lonely roads, I never ran out of gas.

The "So What?" Factor

I didn't want to write my biography. Instead, I wanted to write a book to encourage people to give some thought to their lives and suggest how they could live their lives to the fullest.

The only way I could do that was to reveal some of the lessons I have learned over my years and describe the wisdom I acquired from them. I did it, of course, by experience, which I am told is the best teacher. It's also a pretty tough teacher, doling out a lot of knuckle raps with a ruler.

In these pages, I reveal the many experiences I have had over my lifetime, the things I learned from them, and the ways I believe you can use them as lessons when planning your own life's journey.

Just in case the message doesn't come through loud and clear, I'm including a "So What?" paragraph at the end of every chapter. That's because you may be tempted to say, "Okay, Herb. You did this instead of that in your life. *So what?*"

I'll try to answer this question, even before you ask it, at the end of each chapter.

This way, we can share more easily the lessons I learned over my life. In some cases, these lessons cost me big time, especially in money, and pain.

To you, they're free.

TWO

You Gotta Start Somewhere

The one thing you can't plan on during your journey through life is where you start — geographically, economically, and culturally-speaking.

I started in Russia, where I was born in a town called Barnaul. It wasn't just Russia; it was *Siberia*.

To save you the trouble of looking it up on a map, I can tell you that Kazakhstan is to the West of Barnaul; Mongolia is to the East; and Siberia is to the North. In other words, Barnaul is located in the middle of Deep Nowhere.

If you think "cold" as soon as you hear "Siberia", you're thinking correctly. In winter, my father would wrap my mother's legs in newspaper to keep them warm while he kept moving, performing whatever work he could find to feed his family.

I like to think that the first step I took in planning my life was to scream at my parents to get me the hell out of Barnaul. They responded by taking me to Western Europe when I was three months old and on to Israel two and a half years later.

To my mother and father, Israel represented something that is difficult to describe. The country was just a year old when we arrived and, after the horrors of WWII and the Holocaust, it represented both a refuge and a paradise to my parents.

We might have stayed and helped build the country, but we didn't. It was mostly my father's decision. Born and raised in

Poland, he had gone through the kind of hell that no one should endure. He had served in three armies: the Russian army, the Polish army, and the Israeli army. These armies didn't march around the country to brass bands or spend their time guarding politicians. They were involved in wars, killing perceived enemies, and risking their own lives because the people on the other side were trying to kill them. During WWII, no part of the world saw more intense fighting than Central and Eastern Europe, where my father served in the Polish and Russian armies. Imagine what this does to a man. If nothing else, it makes made him tough.

Actually, my father was a tough guy before he became a soldier. He knew my mother and her family before the war began in 1939, during the years leading up to what represented a decade of suffering for much of that part of the world. Starvation was rampant. No one, except the top brass in Moscow and elsewhere, had enough to eat. They were so hungry that my father and a buddy would creep into farmers' fields at night and dig up potatoes to feed their families and my mother's family. Without those potatoes, the families might have starved. Had my father and his friend been caught, they would have been shot on the spot. They didn't care. You do what you gotta do.

I don't know if it was the stolen potatoes or my father's natural charm, but my mother and her family agreed that he would be good husband material for her. When they married, their plan for their life's journey was based on one decision above all — to get the hell out of the Russia-Poland region and head for Israel.

I was born before they managed to escape Europe. My mother was a wonderful woman, but she had terrible timing; she gave birth to me in the dead of winter. (Wait a minute — maybe the bad timing was my fault!) When she went into labour, my father bundled her up, placed her on a sled, and pulled her three miles through the snow. He kept warm by wrapping layers of newspapers around his feet because he didn't have winter boots. You want to talk tough? That was my dad.

On to Israel

By the time we made it out of Europe and into Israel, my sister Riva was born.

Israel was a lot more appealing, in some ways, than Eastern Europe, as you can imagine. We had a fairly comfortable life there. My father was a good house painter and a hard worker. We lived in a community that shared our dreams and our values. Like virtually all the other Israelis around us, we could have remained where we were and drifted along with the tide.

But my father had other plans for us.

Until he arrived in Israel, his life had been controlled by other people and other events — from the depths of the Great Depression to the horrors of WWII. Once in Israel, those events became distant memories. But the threat of war hung over Israel and still does.

My father was constantly aware of the possibility that conflict loomed on the horizon and that his children would be required to serve in the military. Dad had had enough of military life and of battles, large and small. He didn't want that for his children. He wanted a better life for us than we could count on in Israel. So he planned his life's journey and, along with it, part of mine as well.

I recall clearly the day we left Israel for Brazil. It was the first day — in fact, the only day — I saw my father cry openly. As I said, my dad was a tough guy. If you're of a certain age, you would understand if I told you that watching my father cry was like watching John Wayne cry.

And Then Brazil

We moved to Brazil because my father had relatives there. He also had relatives in Venezuela, but that country was wrapped in political turmoil, and turmoil was something my dad wanted to avoid.

Brazil or Venezuela? Moving to either place would have been a stepping-stone as far as my parents were concerned. Their ultimate goal was, and always had been, to live in North America

— either Canada or the U.S. For reasons I'll explain later, Canada ultimately became our home.

Those of us who live in Canada need to remind ourselves from time to time just how much the majority of people in the world understand and envy us and all that we have, and how much we take it for granted. The freedom, the opportunity, the stability, and the promised future made Canada and the U.S. shining stars all those years ago. Canada remains a shining star, and if it's super-patriotic to brag about the country you live in, then I'm a super patriot.

So Canada and the U.S. were places my parents wanted us to grow up in and consider our homes. Brazil was merely a place to go because my father's cousin lived there.

You might think that having relatives in a foreign country would make it easy for newcomers. It didn't when you didn't speak the language, didn't understand the social customs, and knew nothing about the climate or geography.

It didn't help that my father's relatives saw us not as family members who needed assistance but as pests. They left us on our own, which made things difficult for all of us –especially my father, who naturally saw himself as the bread-winner, the source of our security and comfort.

As a house painter by trade, my father had a skill and he performed it well. It wasn't brain surgery, but he was in demand in the other places we had lived.

In Rio, he wasn't allowed to paint houses. Don't ask me why; it was just a rule, and as new immigrants we weren't in a position to change it. So he was reduced to peddling goods door-to-door. This meant he had to think and act like a businessman, something he had never done before.

As a professional house painter, he knew how long it would take to paint a house, how much he expected to make for a day's work, and how much to fairly charge. But as a peddler, he had to buy goods from a supplier, estimate how much he could sell them for, and be prepared to negotiate prices at both ends. This was a real problem for him because, like me, he had a heck of a time learning Portuguese.

That was his first challenge. The next one came from the way the Brazilians, or at least the ones living in Rio, treated peddlers.

Most of my father's customers lived in the mountains overlooking Rio on steep hills that took a thousand — literally a thousand — steps to climb. Dad did it, carrying his goods with him, in heat that often reached 45°C.

Door-to-door peddlers were generally welcomed in Rio, but they had to follow strict rules. None of the houses had doorbells. None had air conditioning either, so the windows and often the doors were open to catch whatever cooling air might pass through.

The rules dictated that peddlers had to stand in front of each house and clap their hands, waiting for whomever might be inside the house to whistle. A whistle meant the peddler could come inside. If a peddler dared to enter the house or even get too close to the door without hearing the whistle, he could be shot. That's what my father had to go through every day to support his family — climb the stairs with the goods on his back, clap his hands outside each door, wait for someone inside to whistle, and hope with his limited knowledge of Portuguese that he could make a sale.

That was just the beginning. Brazilians buy things differently from most of the rest of the world. Instead of considering the total price of the things they're buying, they think in terms of payments. Everything is priced according to three equal payments. Brazilians judge the price they pay based on the amount of each payment without interest being charged against the balance owing.

When my father made a sale, he collected — if he could — a third of the actual price of the product, knowing he had to return twice to collect the rest of the money. You won't be surprised to learn that when he returned for the balance he would often discover the buyer had moved away, and he could forget about collecting the money owed him.

My mother worked as well, but she had a better grasp of Portuguese than my dad. She was also more aggressive, which

Herb Singer

probably helped us in various ways. Nobody ever skipped a payment owed to my mother — she wouldn't put up with it. Somehow, we managed to survive.

I lived with my parents in Rio from the time I was 12 years old until I turned 14. Living in Rio as a budding teenager whose body was being flooded with hormones might sound like a picnic, with all those beaches and the mountains and the warm weather. But I hated it.

Part of it was the language. It didn't help that I was big for my age, and I was placed in a class of 8-year-old students. For the first few months, I couldn't even communicate with them in English because the only languages I spoke were Hebrew and Yiddish. For a while, I was the big dumb kid who everybody snickered at. It didn't discourage me. In fact, it encouraged me to at least learn the Portuguese language, which I did very quickly so I could understand what they were saying about me.

I endured that kind of treatment for a year and a half. When I turned 14 and was ready for high school, my parents announced that there was no future for me in Brazil. It was still very much a Third World country with all kinds of problems that needed solving, and they decided the Brazilians should take charge of solving them, not their son.

They sat me down and said, in effect, "We want you to go where you have a better chance to succeed than you would have here."

This sounded good to me.

"We've picked two places for you," they said.

One option had me returning to Israel to be with my people. It was an exciting time in Israel, but going back would have meant serving three years in the Israeli army after I turned 18. The other option had them sending me to New York City, where I would attend rabbinical school, become judicious and highly respected, and maybe perform a marriage now and then. Having a rabbi in the family would have been prestigious, I guess, but the idea did not appeal much to my parents, who were not very religious. Studying to be a rabbi, however, meant getting a free education at a pretty good private school and access to America, first for me and later for my parents.

My parents made many sacrifices for Riva and I. Their focus was rarely on themselves, but on their children, whom they wanted to enjoy a life more comfortable, more satisfying, and more secure than their own. I remind myself each day to never forget this; it's my way of honouring what they did for me and what they gave up for themselves.

I wished nothing but good fortune for Israel, but hey — New York City was New York City! It was the Big Apple, full of big opportunities and exciting places to visit: Central Park, Broadway, Times Square, Yankee Stadium, and Wall Street. My parents decided that, all in all, I should head for New York instead of Tel Aviv, and I agreed with unbridled enthusiasm.

I was 14-years-old when I took the long journey North.

I never looked back.

So What?

My father's decision to leave Israel, with the full support of my mother, was the result of taking the long view. They could have remained in Israel and not needed to adjust to their many new challenges, including changing my father's profession, learning a new language, and adapting to a totally different society. No one could have blamed or second-guessed them.

But they looked further ahead — not for their benefit, but for the sake of their children. Many of us don't plan any further ahead than what we're going to eat for dinner today. Making serious decisions, especially those involving the future of your children, means looking beyond today, this week, and this year and deciding what is best in the long run. Your decision may not always be right, but you need to at least consider what you know, weigh the options, and make up your mind.

What do you decide? It's up to you. Just give it a lot of thought, make up your mind, and do it.

Sometimes it's better to make a wrong conscious decision than to make no decision at all.

THREE

Choosing Your Travelling Companion

You may have noticed that human beings come in many sizes and colours, but only two genders. I tend to think that this has a meaning beyond the need for procreation, and that each gender is intended to assist the other in achieving success and satisfaction in life.

I don't want to get into a discussion about the whole hunter-gatherer versus nest-builder debate. That's not my expertise. I think I'm pretty good at other things, however, and one of them is — was? — choosing a mate for life. The bottom line is that it's a damn good idea. Finding an ideal mate, I mean.

You can choose to be a lone wolf and trek through your years without having a permanent relationship with another person. I'm told by people who study these things that social animals who are denied a mate or are banished from the pack tend to have short and difficult lives. Humans are social animals, and a good mate helps us along the journey of life by bringing out the best in us and filling the empty spaces in our being.

When my parents agreed to send me to New York, it was to start me on a life that would be more secure and more fulfilling than their own. That happened, eventually. But the most important part of that move was meeting Rhoda.

The Big Apple

Arriving in New York from Rio was like landing on another planet. I had seen pictures of the city and knew the basics of the place, so I figured I knew what to expect. I knew Manhattan was an island; that the Empire State Building was the tallest structure in the world; and that Wall Street was where millions were made and lost on the stock market. Nothing, however, compared with actually being there.

The skyline was an incredible sight. Rio had lots of stunning natural scenery, but if I had come from the deepest jungle in Africa, I could not have been more amazed at the sight of the New York skyscrapers. The biggest impact on me wasn't the view of the skyline. It was the energy I sensed all around me. This was the place, I knew, where I could become the success I wanted to be, the place where I could harness the power and the confidence to reach whatever goal I set for myself. All I had to do was tap into it, and I would be on my way. And I did.

I had learned to speak passable Portuguese in Rio, but I was never very good at reading and writing the language. Nobody, of course, spoke Portuguese in Brooklyn, and while a lot of people I encountered spoke Hebrew and Yiddish, it was pretty clear to me that the key to getting ahead in America was to speak and write in English. Without English, I would always be an outsider in Brooklyn and, I realized, in the rest of the world.

I arrived in New York on the first day of May 1960. By the first day of August, I could speak, read, and write English. Okay, I wasn't William Shakespeare, but I knew how to understand the people I encountered and get them to understand me. Russia, Israel, Brazil, and all the other places in the world were no longer of importance to me. I understood the source of my father's original goal of reaching North America, and that he had probably planned it as far back as those cold nights when he dug up and stole potatoes to feed his and my mother's family in Russia. Thanks to him, I made it there, and I wasn't going back.

I did have a problem, however. As well as I did in rabbinical school — and I did very well — I couldn't be a rabbi, even if my parents had liked the idea.

It appealed to me somewhat. Hey, it had a lot going for it. Becoming a rabbi would have brought a lot of good things with it, including respect and steady work. But I couldn't do it. I had the school marks to succeed at it. I just didn't have the religious belief for it, which I have been told is a fairly important condition for the job.

So when I finished my high school education, I didn't continue the studies I needed to become a rabbi. I found work during the day and enrolled in studies at New York University at night. This decision, by the way, did not disappoint my parents who, as I mentioned, weren't all that religious in the first place and saw rabbinical school primarily as a means for getting their son through high school at minimal expense. It was also the first step towards getting the entire family to America.

And Then Came Rhoda

I worked at almost any job available to me. Some were interesting, and some were boring. Some paid well, and some were close to slavery. One job, I remember clearly, was working as a car jockey for an automobile rental company. I did so well that they moved me into a job working at the counter for a while. I suppose the thought occurred to me at some point that renting cars could be a business worth considering. If so, I didn't give it much thought because, at the time, my mind tended to be occupied by a petite, dark-haired girl named Rhoda.

Here's how it happened: One Friday, a buddy of mine and I were riding our bicycles in Lincoln Terrace Park, located in the middle of Brooklyn. At the other end of the park, I saw this pretty girl watching some of the other kids play basketball. Something about her fascinated me. I couldn't take my eyes off her. As we crossed the park, I nudged my buddy and said, "See that girl over there? I'm gonna marry her."

Teenagers say stuff like that all the time. Usually they're either dreaming or bragging. I wasn't doing either. Twenty-five years after that day, I was visiting Los Angeles, where my buddy from Brooklyn was living, and I looked him up.

"Remember that girl in the park?" I asked. "The one I said I would marry?"

"Yeah," he grinned. "So what?"

"Well, I did. Marry her, I mean."

I learned the girl's name was Rhoda. We talked a while, she agreed to let me walk her home, and one way or another, we've been together ever since. Rhoda has confessed that she had spotted me long before I saw her in the park that day. She asked around, learned who I was, decided she liked my looks, and promised herself she would meet me some day.

I had been playing drums in the rabbinical school marching band. I didn't expect to become a new Buddy Rich or Ringo Starr or any other big-time musician. I just kept the beat, and I think I kept it pretty well. Rhoda was a pretty good judge of my musicianship because she played the piano and rather well too. She has often said that if my parents could have afforded music lessons for me, I might have had a career playing in bands. Maybe so. I know that I learned something from one of my friends who was the opposite of me, an artsy type with the kind of creative talent I don't believe I had. What I learned was to recognize my abilities and concentrate on them. I might've tried to match him as an *artiste*, but I doubt that I would have succeeded. I had other abilities and chose to develop and apply them instead. *Don't try to be something you aren't*, I thought, which probably isn't news, but it's worth remembering.

Anyway, Rhoda saw me in the band, and after I saw her in the park, everything seemed pre-arranged. Not that I believe in that stuff, but it makes you wonder.

Walking her home that first day, we talked non-stop, and suddenly, I had a beautiful and interesting girlfriend.

Rhoda had been born and raised in Brooklyn and was attending an all-girls school. She was something of a tomboy; she was always ready to play baseball or just get out and enjoy life. She came from a background similar to my own; she was not rich — far from it. Right away, we had something in common: We were fed up with being poor.

Rhoda's father ran a small linoleum business, which he worked hard at maintaining to support his family. Unfortunately, he had suffered from rheumatic fever as a child, and the disease had seriously weakened his heart. Laying linoleum is not an easy job, especially if your health isn't first-rate, and Rhoda's father struggled throughout his life. Eventually he lost his business and had to pick up work wherever he could find it and whenever it was available.

Poverty has a special effect on people. If you have never lacked money to pay for the essentials of life, you can never fully understand the impact that poverty can have on people. Some give up; they were born poor, and they expect to remain that way for the rest of their lives. But not everyone. People who come from poverty and who share the qualities I listed in the first chapter — Ambition, Identity, Vision, and Pride — change in a different way. They grow determined not to suffer from poverty ever again and never to let their children grow up that way.

The struggles that Rhoda's family suffered taught her the importance of financial stability, but not substantial wealth. I was dreaming of mansions with swimming pools and rolling gardens; she was more interested in middle-class bungalows with white picket fences, paying the rent, and buying groceries.

The way I saw it at the time, we both came from nothing so we had to measure our resources in other ways. We had identity, we had love and support from our families, we had each other, and we had an attitude that said we would not be denied the chance to convert our shared visions into reality. Beyond that, we had nothing to lose. Whatever we achieved, it would be better than what we had starting out with.

Rhoda and I talked about these things over and over, eventually agreeing to get married, raise a family, and live a life free from financial worries. It was all pretty ambitious. I was scrambling for whatever work I could find while trying to concentrate on my evening studies at NYU.

Rhoda was working full time as a legal secretary in Manhattan while attending Brooklyn College. Three nights a week, she took courses in court stenography and often rode the subway home late at night. This was the 1960s, a time when New York City was no garden of roses. Crime was rampant, drugs were everywhere, the city supposedly was going broke, and no one could see an easy way out.

Canada!

In the middle of this, one of Rhoda's friends asked her if she would like to spend a couple of weeks in a foreign country. Rhoda thought she meant France or Japan — which would have been out of the question — but her friend wasn't talking about a far off land; she was referring to Canada.

"My aunt moved to Toronto," she explained. "She'd love to have us stay with her for a couple of weeks."

If Rhoda could find $45 for the return airfare, they would be on their way. Rhoda found the money, and they both flew North.

Toronto was a revelation to her. New York was dirty, risky, and crumbling, while Toronto was clean, safe, and burgeoning into an exciting major city.

Rhoda returned to Brooklyn, raving about Toronto. She suggested that after we were married, we should move there because Toronto was far more appealing than New York.

I didn't take much convincing. I had a cousin in Toronto, whom I had never met, but who had sent *C.A.R.E.* packages to our family when we were living in Israel. Rhoda's five-star review of Toronto encouraged me to go and see for myself. I visited my cousin, looked around the city, and agreed with Rhoda — it looked like a pretty good place to live.

I wrote my parents in Brazil to tell them about my marriage plans. They replied that they had been living with "a paper-letter child" for six years. Now they wanted a real son nearby, so they agreed to leave Brazil for Canada. Arriving in Toronto, they applied for residence status, which meant they were not permitted to leave the country until their application was approved. Instead of waiting around for the legal paperwork to get done, we all agreed to move the wedding from Brooklyn to Toronto, and on December 4, 1966, Rhoda and I became Mr. and Mrs. Singer.

Of all the decisions we make in life, it's hard to come up with two that are more significant than getting married and moving to a new country. Rhoda and I did *both* at the same time, and we haven't regretted it for a day since.

The Women I Admire

This is as good a time as any to mention that everything I accomplished with my life was achieved with the energy, assistance, and faith provided by Rhoda. It may be common — but probably not common enough — for men like me to explain that they owe their success to the support of their spouse.

But while Rhoda is an exceptional woman in her energies, intelligence, abilities, and devotion, she would want me to note that the abilities of too many women are ignored by men and sometimes even by themselves.

Some of us males lose sight of the fact that more than half of the world's population is composed of women. So it strikes me now and then that the *other* half of the population couldn't put their socks on in the morning without the assistance of women. I'm not talking about doing laundry; I'm talking about the business abilities of women, many of whom are beginning to show what they can do.

As I write this, three of the largest provinces in Canada have women as premiers. Whatever your politics might be, it's clear that it takes a lot of things, including intelligence, organization, vision, and leadership to reach such a high position. These women have proved they have what it takes to get to the top.

I have no doubt that these same qualities would help women who are striving to move up the ladder in business; many women are just waiting for the opportunity to do so. Will it be easy for them? Probably not. Nothing worth achieving in this life is easy. The biggest hurdle facing most women will be to get past men standing in their way.

So here's my point: If you are a woman reading this — or a man who knows about a woman determined to make the most of her life — don't assume that this book has a MEN ONLY warning on the cover. It's for anyone of any age and gender who thinks, "Maybe this Singer guy will be able to pass along some wisdom that I can use in plotting my life."

Or something like that.

Anyway, the lessons are directed equally at men and women because one gender is just as capable of doing great things as the other.

And no, Rhoda did not ask me to put this in the book.

It was all my idea.

Really.

It Was All About Sandwiches

One more story from that period, and this one has both a moral and a happy ending.

One evening while we were dating, Rhoda had a girlfriend sleep over at her house. It was a Friday night in October, and late the next day, her friend's boyfriend came by to take the friend on a date. He brought along a buddy who planned to join them on their Saturday night date. This guy was impressive. He was a tall and handsome third-year student at Columbia who belonged to one of those exclusive college fraternities that everybody wants to join.

His high-class fraternity was having a dance that evening. The fraternity had booked a famous band, and the night promised to be filled with young people performing all the dance crazes of the day — the Stroll, the Hop, the Locomotion, and other stuff.

Rhoda loved to dance. She especially loved to dance with a good partner who knew all the moves in those dances I mentioned. I was working that Saturday night, and Rhoda called me to ask what I thought of the idea of her going to the dance with this tall, good-looking college fraternity version of Fred Astaire.

It's a measure of my love and trust that I said something like, "Sure, have fun, and tell me about it tomorrow."

From what I hear, the dancing was great, and the guy acted like a perfect gentleman. When the dance ended, he asked Rhoda what she would like to do next. She replied that a friend of hers was in a body cast in hospital, and Rhoda would like to visit her. The college guy asked if he could trail along, and Rhoda agreed.

Later, Rhoda discovered that the whole evening had been a set-up. The college guy explained that he had been admiring Rhoda for some time and, when he heard that his buddy was dating Rhoda's friend, he just happened to tag along in hopes of asking her to the frat dance.

Walking to the hospital in the chilly night air, Rhoda suggested they stop at a cute café she liked for a hot chocolate to warm up. It was a pleasant place, filled with atmosphere — Rhoda was very into atmosphere at the time — but the guy suggested they skip it and go to a coffee shop down the street where the hot chocolate was just the same, he said, but 25 cents cheaper.

Now here's something I have to tell you about me. I'm as generous in many situations as I can afford to be. Always have been. Back then, if Rhoda said she would like a sandwich but wasn't sure what kind, I would bring her four different sandwiches. If she didn't like the pastrami, I thought, maybe she'd like the egg salad.

If she didn't like the egg salad, maybe she'd like the smoked turkey, and so on. It's just the way I am.

Rhoda's mother gave her daughter a lot of advice, as mothers do, and the one bit of advice that Rhoda always remembered was, "Find a man who is always kind to you and stay with him because a man who is kind to you will never hurt you — his heart won't let him."

Walking with the frat boy away from the little café with lots of character towards the tired and dusty coffee shop where most of the patrons went to sober up — all to save two-bits — well, it made an impression on Rhoda. The fraternity fellow's parents were paying his way through university. He didn't have a job, didn't need one, and surely didn't need to worry about saving 25 cents on a hot chocolate for a girl he had been plotting to go out with for years.

Rhoda told me that on the way to the coffee shop all she could think about was me working hard on Saturday nights, buying her four sandwiches when she wanted one, and what this said about being kind. It sure made up for not knowing a few dance steps and having friends in a snobby fraternity!

When the evening was over, and they were at Rhoda's parents' door, the frat boy asked if he could see her again. Rhoda said, "No, thank you," told him she was dating me, and that was that.

I'm not suggesting for a moment that spending 25 cents more for Rhoda's hot chocolate would have changed things. According to Rhoda, it was my attitude towards her, not the stinginess of the college man, that made the difference.

There's a lesson in there somewhere. Unlike the other lessons in this book, I leave it up to you to figure out what it is.

So What?

I guess you can find a happy hermit somewhere, but I don't know any. And some people smile their way through life changing partners the way they change their socks. I often wonder what's behind the smiles. It's tempting and easy when you're young to think of a partner as someone to hang around just for the weekend. Eventually, all those weekends add up, and one day you realize that achieving anything important in life demands something called "commitment".

If you want to do important things in your life, you need to commit to a partner on your journey. Man or woman, straight or gay, none of us can become all that we are capable of becoming without a partner. One of the most important decisions you make on your journey is choosing your partner and supporting each other all the way.

You may have made that decision by now, and you may think your marriage is less than perfect, so maybe you should change partners. That's probably not a good idea. This is a journey, not a dance. If you think your partner is less than perfect, you may be right, but I'll bet you're not perfect either. Maybe you should consider aiming for the same goals, then find a way to make things work.

All those years ago, in that park in Brooklyn, I made a snap decision that I have never regretted. Was I lucky? Am I smarter than I gave myself credit for? I don't know and don't care. I know only that my journey could not have been as rewarding or as satisfying without Rhoda travelling with me.

I hope you're as lucky. Or as perceptive.

FOUR

Dead Ends, Detours, and Heavy Traffic

What happened to the kid who couldn't wait to get out of Rio with its year-round summer weather and perfect beaches? He flew north to Toronto to make his fortune and wound up spending the winter of 1967 lugging luggage on and off conveyor belts in -20°C weather at the airport in Toronto. Had this really been such a smart move after all?

I worked the evening shift, from four in the afternoon to midnight. Rhoda had a job as a legal secretary, heading into the office at nine in the morning and coming home after five in the evening. We hardly saw each other.

Working for Air Canada appealed to me — at first. It was a beginning, and the airline business offered promise to a young guy with a wife and family. It was a glamorous industry, worldwide in scope, and you could make a lot of money. The trouble was, most of the glamour and money went to the pilots and executives. If I wanted to really explore all the possibilities of a career in the airline industry, I would either have to learn how to fly a 747, which didn't seem likely, or work my way through the executive ranks. Few pilots become millionaires, so I looked at moving into a management position with the company, starting with sales. Airlines are big-ticket operations, and I might have been able to pick up enough contacts and knowledge to start a business connected with the industry.

I seriously considered taking that route, until I learned that Air Canada's policy forbade employees from moving into sales until they had at least two years experience in the company. Two years was too long for me to wait, and I began looking elsewhere.

A Born Salesman

One reason I considered a sales position was because it came easily to me — selling, that is. Being a natural sales guy is a very valuable talent to have. Some of us are born salespeople and some of us are able to develop the ability from scratch. Of all the skills you can acquire in life, being able to sell something — including yourself, by the way — should never be underestimated.

People who have the idea that a salesperson is just a guy in a loud sports jacket leaning on a used car or a woman who demonstrates fridges at Sears are limited in their view.

One way or another, we are all salespeople, even when the thing we are selling is ourselves. Every successful person I know has some sales aptitude. Applying for a job, asking for a raise, and almost every interaction you have with your family involves the ability to get the other person to see your point of view and accept it. That's what selling is all about.

I had a knack for selling. More than that, I enjoyed selling. Schlepping baggage at the airport not only failed to match my vision of becoming wealthy; it didn't make use of my selling skills. So I moved to something that did. Something that might have been the toughest sales job you can name.

I sold insurance door-to-door.

If you ever want to appreciate the job you have now, take a week off and try selling something door-to-door. Just to make it even more difficult, try selling something that nobody wants to buy or even think about — like accident and sickness insurance.

I covered much of the province of Ontario in mid-winter, slogging through knee-deep snow, avoiding barking dogs, knocking on doors, interrupting somebody's day, trying to get them to agree to pay me money for protection against something they didn't want to happen. Every time I knocked on a door or launched some small talk with farmers, I knew to expect more rejection than acceptance. Just to make it tougher, sometimes I was on the road five days a week, coming home on weekends. This was not an easy way to make a living.

The insurance company I worked for had been founded and was still being operated by a man named W. Clement Stone. His motto was, "All I want to do is change the world." How's that for ambition? Stone had confidence in himself, partly because he had come so far. He began by selling newspapers on the streets of Chicago as a young boy and moved on to selling insurance door-to-door. When he realized that the way to get wealthy was not to sell the insurance but to own the insurance company, that's what he did. He launched his own insurance firm, calling it *Tthe Combined Insurance Company of America*. He grew it into a billion-dollar-plus company and lived to celebrate his 100th birthday, proving that hard work never hurt anybody. He also gave away a lot of his money to various charities and wrote best-selling books promoting the idea of positive thinking. All in all, he was a pretty successful guy.

For two-and-a-half years, I stuck with Stone's insurance company and his personal philosophy for success. Sales wise, I did pretty well, but Rhoda and I paid a price. Rhoda had trouble sleeping at night while I was on the road, and I developed an ulcer from all the bad food I was eating in greasy spoon restaurants. Finding something that would keep me at home and eating Rhoda's cooking sounded like the best cure for both of our ailments, so I gave up on the insurance business.

Smooth Operator

I needed something that would get me off the road and into an industry that held promise for growth. Looking back, I suppose I could have identified a dozen different businesses to choose from. Would I have done as well as I have with any of them? I don't know, and it doesn't matter. Sometimes you can't pick and choose the perfect option; you just need to identify the best one available. For me, it happened to be a job working with a major car rental company.

I landed a job in Operations, which meant that I had to keep everything moving as smoothly as possible. If you have ever rented a car or truck, most of your contact has been with the staff at the rental counter. They confirm your reservation; check your licence and credit card; have you sign the forms; and hand you the keys. In a well-run company, this looks like a seamless process where everything runs smoothly, and the customer never knows what's going on behind-the-scenes. Nor should they. The customer is interested only in the basics: Is my car ready? Is the price right? Can I go now?

Operations houses the hidden elements of the business, the ones that make sure things are rolling smoothly at the front counter. Cars need to be cleaned, washed, and serviced between rentals. That's easy to grasp. They also need to be positioned according to demand, which varies widely according to the season, the day of the week, and even the time.

Here's an example: In a rental car company, you never want to run out of vehicles for customers, so you need to ensure that cars are in the right place at the right time. Whenever a rental company has no cars available, it hands a sale to its competitor and may lose a loyal customer forever. If your cars are sitting somewhere they're not needed, or if a rental location always has far more cars than it needs to satisfy the demand, you lose money big time. You need to take the cars to where the customers are. Simple, right? Or maybe not.

The biggest demand for rental cars at airports occurs on Sunday, Monday, Tuesday, and Wednesday. That's when you need to have the largest number of cars in the fleet waiting for people to step off their planes and into their reserved vehicles. Later in the week, things change. From Thursday to Friday, the demand for car rentals is higher downtown than at the airport. So on Thursday nights, you move much of your fleet back into the city. Come Sunday night, you get those cars back to the airport again. At the company I was working for, we would move as many as 200 cars between downtown and the airport each week to meet the changing demand.

Operations and the front counter were the places to learn how to run a car rental company. I found the business fascinating. I also could see the things that were working to make the company successful, and the things that could be improved to draw more customers. This, I decided, was a business that I could relate to and identify with, and the opportunity could turn my dreams into reality.

I committed myself to become the best Operations Manager in the business, and maybe I was. But, once again, I learned that everything comes with a price.

The price, as usual, was time. I needed to find a way to spend more time with my family, which meant that somehow I had to expand my opportunity while shrinking the number of hours I was working. At least, that was the idea.

I gave my employer six months' notice, which would give him time to find somebody to replace me, and time for me to train whomever he chose for my job. It would also give me time to figure out what I was going to do next. I loved the car rental business, but I figured I would have to find some other way to be a success.

I didn't walk away from the business, however, because I was offered the chance to stick around in a different capacity. Instead of running Operations, I was given the opportunity to run a sub-franchise in Hamilton, Ontario. It wouldn't be my franchise. It would belong to someone else, but I would run the franchise, as though it were my own. I would do the hiring, firing, and training, and keep the profits after I paid the franchisor his royalties on a percentage basis according to our agreement.

I would be building experience by making management decisions, but I wouldn't be building equity. Essentially, I would be renting the name of the company along with the facilities. The day that the franchising company didn't want me around for any reason — the colour of my tie or because his brother-in-law needed a job — I would be gone. As a full franchisor, I would have had protection from that kind of treatment under the franchise contract. As a sub-franchisor, I had essentially none.

This was something of a concern to me because it meant I would be working primarily for the franchisor. Working for someone else is a way to make a living, but it's not the best way to make your fortune, assuming your fortune is measured in dollar signs with a lot of zeros attached.

Hamilton was a busy city with a lot of industrial activity that has since vanished, but it wasn't Toronto with Big Money and Big Opportunities on every corner. Still, I liked the car rental business; I liked the idea of running things myself, and I especially liked the prospect of spending more time with my family. What didn't I like?

Well, it's complicated.

The Pick Pocket

It had to do with money. Operating a sub-franchise meant I was paying royalties to the franchise owner. The royalties would cover the usual list of expenses; when the expenses went up, my profits went down.

Soon after agreeing to manage the franchise, expenses that I couldn't control began rising.

"Insurance rates are going through the roof," the franchisor told me. "Same with car costs and a dozen other overheads."

Based on our agreement, I had to cover these increases in his costs out of my own pocket.

I'm a trusting guy, and I always believed you should live up to every contract you sign. I had made an agreement to run the sub-franchise, pay royalties to the franchisor, and cover my share of expenses, and I trusted the franchisor to keep his side of the deal. But month after month, I was getting squeezed by the franchisor's tale of rising expenses, and I was working harder to make less money. Based on what I was being told, so was the rest of the industry.

I assumed I didn't have much choice in the matter. A deal was a deal, and if the insurance companies and other outfits were squeezing the franchisor, I'd get squeezed along with him.

This happened until, one day, I attended a business conference that included a lot of other people from the car rental business. Talking with some of them I said, "Boy, the insurance rates just keep going up and up, don't they? Right through the roof."

The others looked at me as though they were waiting for the punch line of a joke.

"What're you talking about?" one of them said. "Our insurance rates have never been lower. They're practically bargain priced."

And the light went on.

One of the reasons the costs I had to cover were going up had been higher insurance premiums. Or so I was told. When I did a little probing, I discovered the other guys were right. Insurance rates weren't rising. They were *falling*. Whenever the franchisor wanted more money, he would tell me, "Herb, insurance rates and a bunch of other costs are going up again. I need more money from you to make ends meet."

In fact, he was double dipping, making money from both the royalties he was charging me and the inflated expenses he claimed I owed. I'm not sure what the legal definition of highway robbery is, but this came close.

For five years, I had worked my butt off to make the franchise a success, opening the place at seven-thirty in the morning and locking it up twelve hours later, seven days a week. Our young son Barry didn't know he had a father. I'd go into his room and give him a smile, and he'd look at Rhoda with an expression that said, "Who's this guy, Ma?"

When the realization sank in, I knew I had to end the working relationship with a guy whom I had trusted to be a straight shooter.

And do what? I could do the thing I knew best. I could run a car and truck rental company. But this time, I would run it for myself and for Rhoda and our kids. Nobody else.

So What?

Now and then you'll read about people who get a business idea, plug it into the plans for their life's journey, and set off to get it done, with no setbacks and no detours. Michael Dell did it when he launched Dell Computers while still in college. In 1971, a guy named Fred Smith got the idea of flying aircraft in and out of a central hub to offer guaranteed overnight courier service. He named his company Federal Express.

Those are encouraging stories for budding entrepreneurs. They're also exceptions. If you're determined to launch your own business during your life's journey, you had better be just as determined to work your butt off to overcome the problems you'll encounter along the way.

Some problems will be caused by your own errors, and some will be caused by the actions of other people. The source won't matter. The response should be the same: Find a way to go around, or drive through them. Just keep going.

FIVE

Risk, Rewards, and Rationale of Starting Your Own Business

Have you noticed how some people can lace up a pair of ice skates for the first time and go gliding away like Wayne Gretzky, while others could skate only if the blades were fastened to their ankles? Do you have a friend who can pull six items from the pantry and turn them into a gourmet meal, while others have trouble making toast?

We all have natural abilities that we're born with. Some people are creative, some are athletic, some are math whizzes, some are linguists. Whatever their talents — and I believe everybody has at least one skill in them, whether they're aware of it or not — they should be treated like gifts to be treasured and used.

One of the gifts some people have is the ability to be their own boss. Along with this knack comes the *need* to be their own boss. Whenever possible, these people use that gift to start a company and grow it to a substantial size with little more than their vision, determination, and work. A lot of work. A lot of *hard* work. These people are called entrepreneurs.

I hadn't given much thought to being an entrepreneur. I knew I wanted to become successful and make a lot of money, but this didn't necessarily mean I would start a company from nothing and build it to a national organization employing thousands of people.

Should your life's plan include being your own boss and launching an entirely new company rather than taking over an existing operation? If the idea appeals to you, do it as early as possible. You need to be smart, you need to be determined, and it really helps to be young and fit, because running your own business is an energy-intensive exercise.

Being an entrepreneur is a state of mind, like being a natural athlete or a natural musician. You don't know how good you are at it until you try it. Trouble is, you can judge how fast you can run by lacing on some shoes and heading for the open road. And you can measure at least the basics of becoming a musician by sitting down at a piano, or choosing a violin, or some other instrument, and listening to the noise you make. Either way, you'll know if the idea appeals to you, and if you have an aptitude for it.

Launching a new business is a little more complicated than picking up a violin. You need capital, financing, licensing, and a thousand other things you won't even know about until you take the first step. And big surprise: It gets more difficult to do with every passing year.

Don't ever believe that being the boss is easy. There are, after all, other ways of having a good life without being the guy who wakes up at three in the morning in a cold sweat because it appears he won't be able to make this month's payroll. If you don't know what that's like, I'll tell you because I've been there. It's hell.

Back to my question: Should you make launching and running your own business part of your journey's plan? Before you answer, here are seven things to ask yourself. If you answer "No" to five of them, I suggest you find a salaried job. If you respond with "Yes!" to most of them, you could be the next Michael Dell. Or the next Fred Smith. Or even the next Herb Singer. Or you could go broke in the first year. (Check Question #2).

1. **Are you honestly prepared to work 80 hours a week?**

   YES [ ]
   MAYBE [ ]
   YOU GOTTA BE KIDDING [ ]

   If your idea of work is a nine-to-five job where you leave your cares at the office and have free time on the weekends, forget about running your own business. In many ways, especially during the early years, the business runs *you*. Real entrepreneurs aren't bothered by this. They may not even see it as a sacrifice because, for the most part, they're enjoying themselves too much. Anyone who has a problem understanding how you could work so hard and have fun doing it is not a serious entrepreneur.

2. **Do you understand that you may not make much money for the first few years of running your business and may even lose money in the process?**

   YES [ ]
   MAYBE [ ]
   ARE YOU SERIOUS??!! [ ]

   Starting a business from scratch isn't like winning a lottery. Rarely do customers stampede into a new business wanting to hand over their money. You could take years to build your company to a size where it pays you a decent profit. Speaking of lotteries, consider these figures:[1]

---

1   SOURCE: *Entrepreneur Weekly*, Small Business Development Center, Bradley University, January 1, 2014

- 25 per cent of all new companies fail in their first year.

- 55 per cent of all new companies fail within five years.

- Nearly half of all new companies fail due to the incompetence of their founder(s). The reasons for failure include: bad pricing policies (too high for the market, too low to make a profit); non-payment of taxes; lack of planning; and poor records-keeping.

3. **Do you have access to enough capital to launch your business and keep it going for the first year or two?**

YES [ ]
MAYBE [ ]
WHAT'S CAPITAL? [ ]

We've all heard about businesses launched on a shoestring that become multi-million-dollar operations. We've also heard of people winning a fortune on a roll of the dice in Las Vegas.

I'm not saying it can't be done, but go back to my point #2 above — the one where I mention that a quarter of all new businesses fail in the first year. If you can't put your hands on the money you need when things go wrong — and something will always go wrong in your first year — you're almost certain to join the one-out-of-four failures.

4. **Are you tough enough to fire somebody if necessary?**

YES [ ]
MAYBE [ ]
CAN'T SOMEBODY ELSE DO IT? [ ]

Everyone I know who runs his or her own company agrees that the most difficult part of the job is telling an employee that they're out of work. And one of the most foolish things you can do is keep someone on the payroll who you can't afford to pay.

I suspect a large number of companies go broke because the people in charge of them do not have the heart to make tough decisions that need to be made. This includes telling someone, who may be doing good work, that they no longer have a job because you have to trim the payroll. Sometimes you have to tell two people they no longer have a job because the other ten to twenty people in the company will all be out of a job if you don't stop losing money.

How do you handle that painful process? You think like a parent who is dedicated to protecting and nurturing an infant child. In my case, Discount became our baby — Rhoda's and mine — and, to some extent, it was also the baby of the people who earned their living from it. The two things that human beings naturally do with babies is nurture and protect them.

That's the way we treated any problem that came up. Sometimes the problem had nothing to do with the Discount staff, and sometimes it did.

Whatever the cause, we had to decide what was best for the "baby" and take action.

You need to learn this skill. If you can't make the hard decisions that are absolutely necessary, you shouldn't be running a business.

5. **Do you know the biggest myths about running your own business?**

YES [ ]
MAYBE [ ]
I DON'T BELIEVE IN MYTHS [ ]

For years, I've been hearing people say how much they would like to run their own businesses, and how certain they are that they'll be successful.

"That's the only way to get really rich," they'll say, thinking of Bill Gates of Microsoft or Ron Joyce of Tim Hortons.

They believe in their success so much that they also begin believing in myths. Beware of anybody who builds his or her future plans around myths, especially myths like these. Not one is close to being true:

- *Your product or service is so great it will sell itself.*

- *The best way to get rich is to start your own business.*

- *Your bank will become your best business partner.*

- *You can build your business by discounting your pricing in the beginning and make a profit by raising your prices later.*

- *You can beat your competitors' prices and still make money.*

- *Your employees will be your friends.*

- *You will have more free time by being your own boss.*

6. **Do you believe it is necessary to always be growing your business, making it bigger, stronger, and more powerful?**

YES [ ]
MAYBE [ ]
CAN WE REST A WHILE? [ ]

Companies are either mice or elephants, and big elephants love squishing small mice. If you can't grow your company large enough to walk with the elephants, you will be stomped on, one way or the other. This is the explanation behind the rule that companies must either keep growing or find a way to keep dodging those elephants by any means available. (You can call it the Charles Darwin approach to business, aka the rule of survival of the fittest.) There is a middle road. You can become large enough and good enough to attract the attention of the elephants, who, instead of flattening you, choose to buy you out. This fills your pocket with capital gains, which are very nice gains to have, as your accountant will explain to you if necessary.

7. **Do you know the most important quality for an entrepreneur to be successful?**

YES [ ]
MAYBE [ ]
A WEALTHY RELATIVE? [ ]

Many people believe a good business education is essential to entrepreneurs, as though an MBA is all you need to be the next Bill Gates. It sure can help, and it does — all of our children have MBAs — but an MBA is more valuable when you're running a business than when you're launching one. That's because MBAs teach you to avoid risk; being an entrepreneur involves embracing risk.

What's more, even the best business educations are ineffective when it comes to providing you with the impetus to get started. Think of the entrepreneurs you have heard of — Bill Gates, Steve Jobs, and, if I may, Herb Singer. None of them/us had a business degree of any kind. If we had, we might have taken a job with an existing business instead of launching one of our own.

What about salesmanship? It sounds like a good talent to have when starting and running a business, and it is. But a lot of very good sales-people would never dream of starting their own company, and the business world is full of stories in which an exceptional salesperson was promoted to a top executive position and flopped terribly. To become a successful entrepreneur, you need more than an education, a concept, and sales ability. You need *passion*.

Of all the qualities necessary to launch a new business and make it work, none is more important, I believe, than a deep desire to succeed. Only people who are truly passionate about their work will reach the limits of their potential. This goes for running your business as much as for anything else in life.

I once read about of a young English boy who, day after day, would lock himself in a room for twelve hours and never come out until he was exhausted from practising his guitar. The guy was more than passionate. He was driven almost to excess. His name was Eric Clapton.

And do you think Wayne Gretzky got up before dawn every winter morning to skate around a local arena or on his family's backyard rink because he liked seeing the sun come up? Or that Serena and Venus Williams hit thousands of tennis balls, millions of times in their careers, because they needed the exercise? They did these things because they were passionate about reaching their goal.

So What?

I don't believe everybody should become an entrepreneur. And I don't believe that choosing not to run your own business makes you less of a success no matter how you measure it.

I have the highest regard for men and women whose plans for their journeys through life involve becoming exceptional at being teachers, artists, musicians, physicians, social workers, plumbers, or experts in any other career. Success can be measured in many ways. I measure it this way: **Success is doing what you want to do.**

I believe that one of the biggest sins in life is being aware of the special talent you were born with and choosing to waste it. If your talent involves launching and running a business, and you have both the energy and passion to make it work, plug it into your plans for your life journey.

If you don't know what you can be passionate about when it comes to setting your goal in life, close your eyes right now and think of one.

Then open your eyes and keep reading, because things are about to get very interesting.

SIX

New Doors, New Challenges

Making up my mind to ditch the franchise I had been running was easy. If I was going to work that hard, I wanted to make myself and my family rich and nobody else — especially not a guy who had been picking my pocket for years. Convincing Rhoda to go along with it, I suspected, would be difficult. On a financial level, we were doing all right, and there was nothing to suggest that we would not be able to continue that way if I had stayed with the sub-franchising deal.

But I refused to continue on that path.

I have always insisted on treating people fairly, and I expect others to do the same. Besides, running a sub-franchise may have been the way to put food on the table and clothes on the backs of our children, but it wasn't the way to reach the level of success I first dreamed about back in Rio. I could only accomplish that goal by starting my own business, which meant risking the comforts we had realized to make a dream come true.

Was it selfish of me to do this? After all, it was my dream, not Rhoda's or that of my children.

Having a good home, a steady income, and healthy children had been Rhoda's dream, and it had come true. Would Rhoda object to my suggestion that we risk it all just to fulfil *my* dream? I feared that she would.

I was wrong. Rhoda had the same concerns about starting our own business as I did. But she agreed with me, and many years later, she explained why.

"You're a very good convincer when you're making your case," she said. (See what I mean about the value of salesmanship?) "And you told me your case was simple. You were angry with the man who had been taking money out of our pockets all those years, and you had no feelings for his company anymore.

"Then you convinced me that you had learned enough about the business that you could start your own company, and we would all do better. You also said the time was right, and we shouldn't wait any longer to make our decision."

I was 35 years old, and I told Rhoda that if I didn't get started with my company, it was never going to happen.

Rhoda understood. She said her mother always told her, "For your husband you travel across oceans, if necessary."

And then Rhoda added, "Maybe that's considered old-fashioned today, but I remembered her words. The way I see it, marriage isn't about taking care of what you need. It's about taking care of what you *both* need. And I realized that you weren't doing this just for you. You were doing it for us. Your family would benefit just as much as you, yourself, if you succeeded."

She was right, as usual. Thinking back about it, I decided that our children would benefit, even if I failed. We wouldn't become an economic basket case if the new company wasn't successful. Rhoda and I both knew I would drive a truck eighteen hours a day if I had to. And maybe we wouldn't enjoy as many perks of life as we had, but our children would learn that it's better to try and fail at something important in your life's journey than never attempt it at all.

You may think it's easy for me to say this after making Discount a success, but I believe it's true.

Here's something else I believe: You learn more from your failures than from your successes.

The Road to Discount

My original plan had been to set up three, maybe four car rental locations in the Hamilton area, making the company big enough to earn us a good living, but staying small enough for me to keep my finger on things. A couple of operations in Hamilton, maybe one in Oakville, and another in Burlington, and I'd be fine.

I knew enough about running a business to recognize that you never become a success by doing the same thing that your competitors are doing. You can, and should, find a way to do things better than them. You also need to make your company distinctive and communicate this distinction to your customers quickly.

Speed was essential. Almost no company makes money in its first year, and almost every start-up operation faces the challenge of having enough capital on hand to survive the early period. The sooner people get to know your organization, understand why it's better, and swing their allegiance to you, the sooner you can get out of the red.

I decided that I wanted my car rental customers to recognize us for two things above all: value and service. "Boy, that was original!" I hear you snicker. "Everybody from General Motors to the local dry cleaner brags about 'value and service'. Lots of luck with *that!*" I wasn't depending on luck. Nobody should ever depend on luck.

We started with the name: *Discount Car & Truck Rental,* which identified our premise for value. My lawyer, among other people, said the name wouldn't work. Renting a car is a big deal to a lot of people, the reasoning went. What was prestigious about "Discount"? It sounds like a bargain basement operation.

Well, I wasn't selling prestige. I was renting cars, and if customers could rent the same car from me as from the guy down the street and get the same service at a discounted price, I believed they would choose me. Over time, they did. And, by the way, there's a little bit of pride in knowing that you're driving a bargain — literally, in our case — and not paying more than necessary.

I ignored the lawyer and others. Discount would be both our premise and our name.

Service was trickier. You can't just promise service; you have to *deliver* it. That gave me an idea. What if we picked up customers at their homes or offices and took them back when they finished renting our vehicles? That's a tangible service that customers can experience, not a promise that they can only hope you'll keep.

At the time, this was considered a wild idea. Pick customers up and take them back when they return the vehicle? Who needs that expense? It would cut our margins significantly.

We didn't need the extra cost, but we needed the distinction that said, from the very beginning, "We're the new guys in town, and here's how we're different."

We also threw in a lot of other things, including good rates, clean cars, and friendly service people.

On its own, the pick-up-and-delivery idea established us as a serious player in the business. Other car rental companies had talked about doing this, but nobody had chosen to do it. The customers, of course, loved the idea. That gave me one of the best rules for building a business: *Always try to do what your customers want, and what your competitors resist offering.*

The idea of picking up customers is no longer considered revolutionary because one of our major competitors makes a big deal about picking you up (but they won't bring you back).

We were the first to offer it. Being the first to do anything is a major achievement. Being the second person is nothing much. I'll prove it: I bet you know the name of the first guy to walk on the moon. Neil Armstrong, right? So what's the name of the second guy to do it?

See what I mean?

Next I found the perfect location for my first office — right across the street from the sub-franchise I'd been operating for years; the place run by the guy who allowed me to line his pockets without me knowing it.

After I left that job, the owner began handling the franchise on his own. Once we were established, I imagined that I would be able to look out my front office window, across the street, and into his eyes. But I didn't plan on it. I wanted to be too busy renting cars and running my business to stand around staring at him.

Ironically, as time passed I noticed that he spent a lot of his time watching Rhoda and me and our staff serve customers who could have gone through his front door if we weren't there. Why did they come to us instead? For the usual reasons any company does better than another. Better price. Better value. Better service.

All of that came later. For now we had a name, a business plan, a location, and something advertising people call a Unique Marketing Proposition.

What didn't we have?

Cars.

Bad Timing

The year was 1980. It was not exactly the time to launch a new company. Interest rates were nudging 23 per cent. OPEC was threatening to shut down their oil wells; there were line-ups at gas stations in the U.S.; unemployment levels were close to 15 per cent; and prices everywhere were rising like hot-air balloons. About the only things that remained low were people's expectations that the situation would improve soon. As I said, it wasn't exactly the time to launch a new company.

There were other challenges as well.

Normally, my nest egg, which I had sunk into the new company, wouldn't have been nearly enough to start something as capital-intensive as a car rental operation. But these weren't normal times, which made things even more difficult. Fortunately, I had another asset that almost made up for any shortfall in cash: my credibility.

Over the years I operated as a sub-franchisee, I had dealt honestly with everybody. If anyone had a problem with me, I found a way to handle it fair and square. Bills were paid on time, and banks were kept up to date on my financial situation. People knew I kept my promises. They trusted me, and their trust was as valuable an asset as I could ever hope to own.

You can buy practically anything you want in life if you have enough money, but you can't buy a good reputation. It needs to be earned, and the longer you earn it, with the more people you encounter, the stronger it becomes.

Rhoda and I earned our reputation with honesty and hard work, and if the idea of promoting those two concepts is old-fashioned, then I'm as old-fashioned as you can get.

When we began talking to people whose support we needed to get Discount started, many reacted with a nod of the head, and the question, "What do you need?"

I used our credibility like cash. In some ways, it was better than cash because, after I used it, I hadn't spent it; it was still in my pocket.

One problem I faced in starting a new business that based on renting cars and trucks involved a non-compete clause I had signed as part of my agreement with the guy who had been picking my pocket for years. Under the agreement, I could not run a car rental firm that competed with him in the same market. So I didn't. Rhoda did. Her name was on the company charter. Mine wasn't.

I worked the front desk. Rhoda was in the back, directing operations and dealing with suppliers. When we needed to discuss something important, we would meet near the coffee machine. She'd ask what I would do in a particular situation she encountered, I would tell her, and then she would agree it was a good move. I would go back to the counter, and Rhoda would see that things got done.

Of course, none of this could happen without cars to rent, and this is where the world's economic problems at the time actually helped us.

The Chrysler Connection

I began acquiring cars by contacting a guy I knew at Chrysler Credit, the arm of the company that provided financing for Chrysler-made cars. When we met to talk about my new business, I laid everything out for him. I told him I needed forty cars to get started. I had a business plan, a good location, a unique marketing strategy, a lot of experience, and a reputation for paying my bills. What I didn't have was money to pay for the cars. I asked if he could help me.

To my surprise he said, "What the hell. You're starting out new, and we're both going to go broke, so why not?" Just like that, we did a deal.

As the smallest of the North American car companies, Chrysler had been battered through the 1970s from two sides. General Motors and Ford were stealing its market share, and imports from Japan were taking sales from everybody by building good quality cars at a price Detroit couldn't match. Many people, including my guy at Chrysler Credit, figured the company wouldn't be around for long.

Then, a stroke of luck. In a brilliant move, Chrysler hired Lee Iacocca to run the company in 1978. Iacocca had made a splash while running Ford. As an example, he was the key guy behind the development and introduction of the Ford Mustang, the car that totally revolutionized automobile design and made Ford billions of dollars. Everybody in the industry admired what Iacocca had done at Ford except for their Chairman of the Board, a guy named Henry whose last name happened to be Ford. Whatever reason Henry had for not liking him, Iacocca was sent packing from Ford, only to be hired by Chrysler.

If there has been a better, more effective, and more influential businessman walking this Earth during my lifetime, I don't know who it might be. Iacocca had the right combination of vision, spunk, and aggression to turn around a massive, ailing company like Chrysler and influence the entire automotive industry in North America.

His motto was, "It can be done," and with him it wasn't all talk. Whatever needed to be done he did it, over and over.

When Iacocca arrived at Chrysler, he realized that the company made too many different cars and used too many different parts building them. Chrysler needed a new line of cars that used common parts; cars that could be sold at a low cost to counter the Japanese imports. He also wanted cars that burned less fuel in response to widespread concern that the world's oil reserves might not last until the end of the century. The new line was designated K-cars, and they saved Chrysler every bit as much as the Mustang benefited Ford.

Chrysler's line of K-cars began with the introduction of the Plymouth Reliant and Dodge Aries. Later, the company introduced the Chrysler LeBaron and Dodge 400, based on the same platform. In 1984, Chrysler introduced the new concept of mini-vans, which revolutionized the entire industry.

The seven-passenger Dodge Grand Caravans, the ones you see rolling along highways in North America, are all direct descendants of the original K-cars, and that's a tribute to Lee Iacocca's vision and his management ability. It's also why, to this day, Lee Iacocca tops my list of all-time heroes.

Iacocca and his designers liked to keep things simple, and their formula for success worked. The K-car engine was a four-cylinder design. It produced 86 horsepower (HP), which was not much but it was a beginning. Later models, with fuel injection and other improvements, produced as much as 200 HP. On the inside were two bench seats, making the cars capable of carrying up to six people, qualifying them as mid-sized cars and not compacts.

The cars ran well, were easy to service, and cheap to buy. Within a few weeks I had a company, a name, a unique sales proposition, and 40 brand-new K-cars to put into customer's hands in exchange for their credit card imprint. We were on our way.

On November 1, 1980 we turned on the lights, opened the doors, and told the world we had arrived.

If I Knew Then...

I've been asked, "If you knew then what you know now, would you have still launched Discount the way you did?"

My answer is, "Probably not."

Who would launch a capital-intensive business like renting cars and trucks when the juice you're paying the banks for the vehicles is running at 23 percent a year? Who would commit themselves, under those circumstance, to working three years, for fifteen- or eighteen-hour days, without making a profit? Looking back from today's vantage point, the whole idea sounds crazy.

It's a little like deciding to go on a diet while everybody around you keeps handing you food to eat, and every TV show has fast-food commercials telling you to super-size your order. Distractions are everywhere in life, which is why you need to set your own goals and decide just how badly you want to meet them. But I believe strongly that if you want to meet your goals badly enough, you'll come out on top.

Nobody knows as much as they need to know before making a decision to launch a business. What can possibly replace your lack of knowledge about all the challenges you are about to face? It's your passion to succeed and your drive to fulfil your dreams. Together, they provide the power to push a lot of barriers out of your way. That's what I had. That's why I ignored some of the chilling facts that might have otherwise persuaded me to give up the whole idea.

But let's face it — I had never planned on launching and running a car rental business. The only plan I had was to become sufficiently successful and wealthy that I would never have to worry about keeping a roof over the heads of my family and putting food on the table for them. Naturally, I wanted to go further than that if I could. But it wasn't the car rental business that worked for me as much as it was my own drive to succeed. I might have started in another business with similar potential, a business that I knew how to operate. It might have been a candy company, a chain of convenience stores, or a computer service operation, who knows?

Not knowing the odds against me was a blessing in disguise. If somebody had told me back in 1980, "Herb, here's what you're going to have to do; here's what you're going to put up with; and here are all the risks you'll be taking," I might have changed my mind. But no one did.

I surprised a lot of people, including myself, I guess. I know I really surprised the guy who had been picking my pocket all those years when I ran his franchise for him. When word about my plans got back to him, he reportedly said, "Singer's going to run his own company? He'll flop for sure!"

Someday, I told myself, I gotta thank him for giving me, with those words, all the motivation I needed to succeed. Seriously. I planned to shake his hand, pat him on the back, and say, "Without your words, I might never have achieved my goal."

I haven't got around to it yet.

So What?

Every time you make a major change in your life, someone will find a reason for you not to do it. Sometimes the person who comes up with the list of reasons why you won't succeed is yourself. If this happens, listen to your inner voice, carefully weigh the odds, and then ask yourself if you are still fully committed to succeed. If the answer is "yes", tell your inner voice to take a hike and keep moving forward.

I'm not suggesting you do anything so foolhardy or impulsive that it's likely to put you and your family in debt for years. I'm talking about developing a plan, working out the details, weighing the pros and cons, discussing it with your life partner, measuring your passion, and deciding to get it done. It's easy to find a reason not to take the first step. And it's only human to believe that taking that step risks stumbling and falling on your face. But do you know any other way to move ahead?

I had maybe a dozen reasons not to start Discount. The economy was terrible. Interest rates were at record levels. I was stretching my assets and credit rating to the limit. I knew a lot about renting cars and trucks, but I had never run a company on my own before. I was taking a risk by offering to pick up customers and to return them at my expense. I could fill the rest of this book with reasons not to start my company.   Fortunately, I had things on the other side of the ledger to balance them.

One was Rhoda's support. She had contributed as much as I had to making the deal with the greedy franchisor work, and I knew she would do the same or more for our own company. Another was my energy level. I had worked eighteen-hour days for some other guy. I knew I would work even harder for myself.

Finally, I had vision and determination. Okay, I agree: Vision, determination, and a buck or two will get you a coffee at Tim Hortons. Forget the coffee. Put your vision and determination to work on something that is important to you, something that represents the best route for your life's journey, and you've made the correct decision.

*I'm not saying you'll succeed every time. But the best way to ensure you **never** succeed is to never try.*

Or, as Woody Allen put it: 80 per cent of success is just a matter of showing up.

SEVEN

Know How Things Work

When a customer rents a vehicle from Discount, they don't know what goes on between the time they tell us they need a car or truck and the time they drive away in it. They don't *need* to know. Everything should move smoothly, so that it appears as though each customer is the only person to rent a car from our entire company at that moment. No matter how many hoops we may jump through to see that the customer gets what they want, our efforts should be invisible. That's the mark of a truly professional operation.

Even when the problem stems from a customer's actions, such as not bringing a vehicle back when promised and leaving us without the car we had planned for the next customer, our policy is to make a smooth adjustment. We may gnash our teeth over inconsiderate actions and apply a legitimate charge where warranted, but I insist that we always maintain our professionalism. In a nutshell, here's our philosophy on customer service:

> *The customer may not always be right.*
> *But the customer is always the customer.*

I have a musician friend who gets upset when he's at a concert and sees someone grimacing while playing a guitar, violin, piano, or any other instrument, as though the player is undergoing a root canal instead of making music for the enjoyment of the listeners.

"You know how to spot the best musicians? They're the ones who focus on the music and not on dramatics," my musician friend says. "They look relaxed, no matter what they're playing at the time. Whether the music is a breeze or nearly impossible to play, they always look the same — cool, confident, and professional. Theatrics don't make the music sound any better, and sometimes they tell you that the player is not a master of their instrument."

I like to think everyone at Discount is a master of the car rental business, or at least their end of it. They avoid getting flustered, never express their annoyance or disappointment to customers, and find a way to enjoy their work. This was our approach from the beginning, and it is even more vital to us today because it sets us apart from everybody else.

Almost every time I open the business section of a newspaper, I read about somebody who says it's hard to become a success in business today. But hey — it has *always* been hard to make a success in business, and the only way to keep it from getting more difficult is to maintain your focus on the customer. The day you treat your customers with less service and respect than they think they deserve is the day your business starts to decline. I haven't seen statistics on the subject, but I'm convinced that as many businesses suffer equally from tough competition and from bad customer service. You can't control your competitors, but you can always control the quality of your customer service. I'm amazed how some otherwise successful people seem to forget that principle of business.

I don't know much about women's yoga clothing, but I know that a company called Lulu Lemon couldn't seem to do anything wrong until the guy who founded the business blamed the customers when his products started to fail. It had something to do with the company's yoga pants becoming transparent, which strikes me as being a serious flaw. Instead of agreeing that the company had a problem, the founder and CEO blamed the physiques of some of his customers. I think he said something about their thighs being too heavy. His attitude was, "We won't change our product; the people who buy them have to change their bodies."

Can you believe he was surprised at the backlash? His customers reacted with their purses and their feet, closing their wallets and walking out of the stores.

I'll be damned if I'll discuss the state of women's thighs in this book or anywhere else. My point is that the guy didn't show respect for his customers. He didn't treat his customers the way he would expect to be treated himself.

Is there a cost in going an extra step or two, not only to avoid insulting your customers, but to offer more service than they expect? Sure there is. But if you don't offer your customers service and respect, the cost is a hell of a lot higher. It's called bankruptcy.

It's All About the Customer

The best way to ensure good customer service is to choose employees who believe in the idea in the first place. Among all the qualities we look for in new employees, none is more important to us than an attitude that says, "I like people, I enjoy working with them, and I'm going to treat everybody I do business with exactly the way I would want to be treated."

You can't preach that kind of religion and expect people to follow it on your say-so. And you can't be phony about it either. You either believe it, or you don't. I believe it, and I have always believed it.

My son, Jay, and I take trips across the country now and then, dropping in on franchises and corporate branches to say hello, shake a few hands, and maybe go to lunch with the manager. It's not an inspection process. It's an opportunity to let employees know that the people back at Head Office aren't just names on a memo or voices on the telephone. They're real people with a sincere interest in the way the business is being operated everywhere in Canada.

On one of these trips to a branch, I arrived on a particularly busy day. Several customers had been late bringing their cars back, which meant the staff who clean, wash, and service them were having a problem keeping up with the demand. They were scurrying like crazy to get cars ready for customers who were lining up at the counter.

I hate seeing customers waiting. They shouldn't have to stand around, biding their time, no matter what the cause. So I took off my jacket and started washing cars myself. The staff couldn't believe it. "Herb's out there washing cars!" they said to each other. Some took pictures.

Did I do it so people would take pictures of me? No. I did it because every customer who had to wait too long for their car would have had a lower opinion of Discount. Not a lower opinion of Herb Singer. They don't know who the hell I am. It was their opinion of the company that mattered, and if I could give it a boost, why shouldn't I? That's the attitude I've been talking about. By the way, Jay takes similar trips to branches and franchises and has often pitched in, like I did, to get cars ready.

Sometimes, job applicants at our company automatically eliminate themselves as prospective employees by having the wrong attitude — like the young woman who lived in Scarborough, which is about thirty kilometres from our office. She had applied for an accounting position, and she was doing fine until she said, "By the way, I live on the other side of the city, so don't count on me coming to work on a stormy day." The inference was that she considered it too much trouble to drive through bad weather or ride public transit if the air was too cold, the wind was too strong, or the snow was too deep. We suggested that she, in turn, shouldn't count on getting a job offer from us.

I don't expect unusual sacrifices from employees, or even perfect punctuality on stormy days in Toronto. That wasn't the point. It was her attitude that made us turn down her application.

Next, we look for good communication skills. Can the new prospect explain themselves well in writing and in conversation?

It is important for all our staff to make themselves understood in a friendly, helpful manner.

Education is also important, but not for the usual reasons. Graduating from high school, vocational school, or at the college level, tells us the applicant has the discipline to tackle a job and complete it. These two measures of education and attitude qualify a prospect for the next level, which is a total background check on employment records and any criminal convictions.

By the way, one thing that is unimportant at Discount, and never will be important as long as I and my family are associated with the company, is an employee's racial origin. Anybody in business who either favours or rejects employees on the basis of the country of their birth, the colour of their skin, the values they treasure, or how they spell their name, is a fool. Racism isn't just wrong; it's dumb. If you walk through our Head Office or any of our corporate branches, you might believe we hire people through the United Nations. We don't. We choose our employees, deal with our customers, and favour our suppliers based on everything *except* their origins and beliefs. I wish all the businesses and professions in the world did things the same way. But they don't.

If job applicants pass the tests I mentioned, we send them to school. It's our school. We call it *Blue & Green University*. New employees attend classes to learn how the system works, and how to deliver the kind of customer service we expect from them. They have to pass examinations before they are assigned full-time jobs, and for the first several weeks of their employment with us, they are paired with mentors whose job it is to answer their questions and measure their abilities.

This is unusual in our business, maybe even unique. The usual choice is on-the-job training, putting new people behind the counter after a few hours watching others at work. That's not good business practice. When customers arrive at our front desk, they don't want to stand waiting while some supervisor explains to a trainee how to complete a rental form. Customers shouldn't have to watch a rookie follow instructions or learn how to use a computer program. They want to be told their car is ready, confirm that the price is what they expected, and get the keys in their hands. So we don't assign rookies to the job. We use university graduates. Okay, it's *our* university, but you get the picture.

We take the same approach with managers. Telling someone that he or she is now a manager doesn't make them a manager. It's a new job that demands different skills, and it's better for the manager to learn the skills in a classroom instead of in front of customers.

The More You Know

The more you know about the way things work, in whatever endeavour you choose, the better equipped you are to do things differently, and do them better.

For example, I knew how the car rental business treated auto insurance companies, and I saw a way to improve on it. Insurance firms need cars for their policy holders to drive while their cars are being repaired. The natural solution for insurance companies was to approach car rental firms and work out deals that were good for both sides.

That's fine, as far as it goes. But I also knew that while the insurance companies needed cars year round, the big car rental companies were only interested in dealing with them from February through April, when the airport rental business was slow. The rest of the year, they treated insurance companies like pests.

Being your friend for just three months of the year is not the best way to build a good relationship. So we let the word out that we were serious about dealing with the insurance industry all year round, and we set up systems to make it easier for them to get the cars they needed. Over time, when they saw we were committed to the insurance industry every day, twelve months of the year, we acquired more and more of their business.

And here's the story behind that story:

We had two customers in this end of the business. Sure, the insurance companies were paying us for the cars used by their policyholders, but they weren't the only ones who deserved our attention. The people who needed our cars had recently been in an accident. Whether it was a minor fender bender or a more serious collision, many were still upset about it, and could use a little empathy and reassurance. Some may never have rented a car before. They appreciated someone taking them by the hand and saying, "We'll make this process as easy as possible for you, because we see this every day and we understand what you are going through. We will even set things up to bill your insurance company directly, so all you have to do is drive away."

How often do you think policyholders would express their appreciation to their insurance company for this service?

How good do you think this made the insurance companies feel about dealing with us?

And who do you think the policyholder would choose when it came time for them to rent a car?

Our relationship with the insurance companies is just one example of how to use your knowledge to gain an advantage in business. If you can look at things from a perspective that's different from companies chasing the same buck as you, you're ahead of your competition.

Here's my final hint on this subject:

Never take your eyes of the customer and what he or she needs and appreciates.

Company Secrets

Like most businesses, the vehicle rental business is more complex than our customers think. Of course, they don't *need* to think about it. They just need their car ready at the right price and the right time. Then they hit the road, maybe with a smile on their face, maybe not.

Here are some facts that you probably never considered and never realized about car rentals. I'm not revealing them to encourage you to start your own car rental company. They're here because, if plotting your life's journey includes running your own business, there is no such thing as useless information. You never know what you may pick up from one company's experience, whatever kind of business they're in, that you can use in your own business.

I may be giving you some tips that you can use to save money when renting your next car from us or anyone else. You know what? I'll take the risk, because I think educated consumers make the best customers. The customer who knows what it takes to meet their level of satisfaction has a greater appreciation for good service.

First, the obvious. If you want to rent cars to the public, you need cars on hand. Lots of cars. On any given day, about 35,000 cars and trucks are in our inventory. When you're acquiring that many vehicles, you're positioned to strike a deal with the manufacturers to get the best possible price. But some manufacturers, believe it or not, aren't interested in making fleet sales.

The two most popular car brands in the world, Honda and Toyota, are not enthusiastic about making fleet sales with car rental firms like Discount. They'll do it from time to time, but according to their needs, not ours. When sales are slow through their dealers, Honda and Toyota talk deals with rental operations. But when customers are pouring into their dealerships, Honda and Toyota tend not to return our calls. They don't want to do business with us. And even when they do business with us, they set a limit in terms of the number of cars they're interested in selling at fleet discounts.

Toyota, for example, doesn't want more than 8 percent of their business going to fleet sales. If they move 100,000 Toyotas through their dealer network in a year, they'll make just 8,000 available to rental companies. Why? Because limiting their fleet sales helps to elevate the price of used Toyotas (and Hondas, which have the same strategy), and that translates into lower depreciation rates for their cars. The lower depreciation levels for Hondas and Toyotas are a reason for their high new-car sales levels, year after year. It's not the only reason, of course; they are very well-built cars. But by controlling the number of used cars flowing out of car rental firms into the market, the auto manufacturers help keep resale prices high and the depreciation levels low.

That's their policy and their strategy, and they have their own rationale for doing business that way. But it's difficult to rely on companies that jump in and out of the market according to their need, or that set a quota on the number of cars they're willing to sell us at fleet prices. That's a good reason for car rental companies to favour products from Ford, GM, and Chrysler.

The Big Three companies have had an incentive to talk fleet sales with us whenever we were ready. In fact, they needed the fleet sales, desperately. Under the deal they had with the auto workers' union Ford, GM, and Chrysler were required to pay 95 percent of the union workers' income when the plants were shut down due to low sales volume. This meant the manufacturers were always looking for ways to keep the plants running, even if they had to sell the vehicles at cut-rate fleet prices.

Things changed after the economic crisis of 2008-2009, when GM and Chrysler came within a whisker of going bankrupt. Now they play hardball with the assembly workers. If the plants don't produce cars efficiently enough, and if the sales from that plant aren't strong enough, they'll close down the plants and walk away. The Big Three don't need Detroit, or Windsor, or any other factory location on this continent as much as they once did. It's a surprising fact to many people that GM manufactures and sells far more cars in Europe and Asia than in the U.S. and Canada. They actually sell about twice as many Buicks in China as in North America and make a lot more money per car from those sales.

Still, car companies have at least a passing interest in selling to us at lower fleet prices because every rental of their cars is a test drive of sorts. You may never have considered buying a new Ford

Fusion, but if you rent from us, and like it, you've taken a step towards visiting a Ford dealer. Selling you one is not a sure thing, but it's an opening that the car companies like to exploit.

When it comes to negotiating with car manufacturers to get the best fleet prices, things become interesting. I don't want to give away secrets, but consider this: If GM tells you as a retail customer that they're offering $3,000 cash off the list price of a new Chevy Malibu, how much do you think they'll lower the price when I say, "I'll take 4,000 Malibus in assorted colours, and can I have them by the end of the month, please?" General Motors makes a profit knocking $3,000 off the Malibu they sell you, and they'll still make a profit by lowering their price for the 4,000 cars we would be willing to buy.

Let me take things a little further and explain some simplified accounting information where renting cars is concerned.

We turn over our inventory of cars about every fourteen months. It's the only way we can guarantee that our customers drive up-to-date vehicles. The biggest secret to making money in the car rental business is timing and price — *when* you sell the cars and *how much* you get for them. Do it right, and you're on solid ground financially. Do it wrong, and you're swimming in red ink.

Once a week, the Discount team assigned to make fleet replacement decisions gets together to review the strategy. They balance what's best for customers when it comes to vehicle appeal and availability and what's best for us to keep our sales and margins healthy.

We make our decision to sell cars based on time of the year, mileage levels, and the state of the used car market. If the market is hot for a particular model and year, we'll check the mileage on cars in our inventory and maybe put them on the auction block.

Sometimes, events affect our decision about making fleet purchases. When Toyota got into hot water in 2012 over warranty problems, people became less enthusiastic about owning one of their cars. We held onto the few Toyotas in our fleet, riding out the manufacturer's problems, until people felt better about them again and prices resumed to their normal level. We are also concerned about replacing the vehicles we put on the used car market. If the new car market is hot, and we have a problem getting the fleet prices we need, we may delay things.

All of these decisions are based on standard business formulas and figures. Like these:

If we buy a car for $15,000, we expect it to earn us maybe $1,100 a month. We'll depreciate the car at 2 percent a month, plus interest. Let's call it $300 a month. After a year in our fleet, we've lowered the value of the car by (12 x $300) or $3,600. Now the car that we paid $15,000 to buy is on our books as an asset worth $11,400.

If we can sell that car for $12,500 instead of $11,400, our cost of owning that car drops by $1,100, or about $90 a month. Now the car has cost us just $210 a month against the $1,100 a month that it brought in from rentals. Does that mean we pocket about $900 a month in profit? Not a chance. We still have to pay salaries, overhead, rental, advertising, maintenance, and a lot of other expenses to keep the cars running smoothly and looking great.

Those are the standards we use to price our business, but nothing is carved in stone. Sometimes, if we make an exceptional deal on our fleet purchase, the car costs us nothing. Other times, for other reasons, we may lose money when we sell the car.

That's how the business works. Each car is an investment on our part. That's easy to understand. Multiply the deal I described by 35,000 and you get an idea of the scope and importance of making good deals on our fleet purchases. A few dollars here and there can make the difference between winning and losing.

Going Global

This is one reason why I resisted moving Discount into the United States market, despite suggestions from a lot of people who believed it made sense. I'm all in favour of expanding the business, but entering the United States would put us up against people like Enterprise, which owns National and Alamo and buys 1.2 million cars a year. With that kind of volume their purchase costs are much lower than we could ever negotiate, putting us at a major disadvantage.

We've also been burned a little when we made an effort to expand beyond Canada. It took us ten years to accept the fact that it was a bad move.

Part of the problem was distance — we tried to work with a franchisee in Australia. Given all the ways that people and businesses can keep in touch with one another these days, you might think that working smoothly with a partner twenty thousand kilometres away would be easy. Well, it wasn't.

Truth is, we made the decision to enter Australia in 2003 as a defensive move. At the time, Australia's trademark laws were so weak that anyone with a lawyer and a few bucks could call themselves almost anything they wanted. Sometimes, it went to extremes. When General Motors tried to launch their company in Australia, they discovered that somebody in that country had already registered the name "General Motors" and refused to give it up. No matter how widespread the GM name was outside of Australia, they couldn't use the name, so GM became known as Holden there.

When we were approached to launch Discount in Australia, we thought it would be a good way to defend our trademark and expand our business in a new direction. We worked at it for ten years before realizing that we didn't have a good fit with the person running things, and we couldn't exert the management control we wanted from the other side of the world.

It didn't work out, but you know what? There are no guarantees in life or business. Accept that, and remember what I said earlier about learning more from your failures than from your successes.

Our experience in Australia didn't turn us off reaching beyond Canada. We just did it in a different manner. In 2013, we completed a deal with Europcar out of France. Europcar operates more than 200,000 vehicles at nearly 300 locations in 143 countries in Europe, the Middle East, Africa, Latin America, the Caribbean, and across Asia Pacific. We have a reciprocal agreement with them. Customers of Europcar can book vehicles from us, through Europcar, and we'll make arrangements for our customers who want to rent cars anywhere Europcar does business. It's a little more complex than it sounds, but it's proof of my point that companies have to keep expanding or risk being squashed by bigger guys. Sometimes you expand like McDonalds, by putting one on every corner, and sometimes you expand by arrangement. We prefer arrangement.

Fleet Street

I'm often asked if it's a good idea to buy a car from a rental fleet. I can't speak for the other guys in the business, but when it comes to acquiring a car from our fleet, I answer with a definite "Yes!" (Actually, the same goes for other quality rental companies. I'm just a little biased here. Can you blame me?)

Okay, you would expect me to say that. But here are my reasons.

First, Discount cars have been maintained strictly according to the manufacturer's guidelines. I would venture to say they are at least as well maintained as privately owned cars. Why? Because our fleet is our most valuable asset, and every business person knows that assets need care and protection.

Second, maintenance on the cars is performed by professionals. They won't skimp on what needs to be done.

Third, cars made today are far more reliable and precise than those made a few years ago. We can thank the Japanese and the Koreans for much of this change; they forced the other manufacturers to catch up. After 50,000 kilometres, most cars today are practically brand-new as far as reliability is concerned, especially if they have been well maintained.

Finally, former rental cars can be available at a better price than privately purchased vehicles. We pay less to acquire them, and we depreciate them fairly. So right off the top, the price should be lower to you. I say "should be" because most of our cars are sold through independent used car operators, and they'll set the best price they can get. It's up to you to haggle. With a former fleet car, you usually have more room to bargain.

So What?

Where does your job fit into the plans for your life's journey? Do you want to start and run the whole show? Or do you want to fit into a niche in some business or profession, where you feel comfortable, and where you can measure your own success on your own terms?

Whichever role you take, always be aware of your customer and what they expect of you. As soon as you lose sight of their expectations, you risk moving down a slippery slope and find yourself sliding away from all the satisfaction and achievement, you're capable of reaching.

It helps, by the way, to enjoy and appreciate people. If you're a cynical hermit, you'll never understand the personal satisfaction from dealing with a customer who honestly appreciates the way you do business. And even if you don't deal with customers directly (and you should, from time to time, to understand their needs and expectations), you will probably deal with staff and suppliers. Both groups will put extra effort into things when they're working for people whose company they enjoy. Believe it or not, this is still news to some folks.

My father, mother and me when we were still in Siberia where I was born. As you can see, I'm already looking for a way out of there.

Herb Singer

Chrysler shipped me 40 K-cars on credit to get Discount started in 1980. The company figured it and me were both going broke at the time, so what did they have to lose.

BRIAN DEXTER / TORONTO STAR

TOUGH COMPETITION: The big boys of car rental business couldn't keep Herb Singer out.

Discounting risks led to success

By John Picton
TORONTO STAR

It was a hectic life.

Herb Singer was working 20 hours a day, seven days a week, trying to get his new company off the ground.

Thinking BIG

A regular series about entrepreneurs

His wife, Rhoda, worked right along with him, taking the kids to school in the morning, picking them up in the afternoon, giving them dinner — then heading right back to the office.

That was in 1980 and the following years, when they were entering an already crowded and cutthroat market to take on such household names as Hertz, Tilden, Avis and Budget.

Today — that market is estimated to be worth $1 billion a year in Canada — their company, Discount Car and Truck Rentals, has sales of more than $50 million a year, has 500 employees, and a fleet of thousands of cars and trucks stretching across Canada and as far south as Greensboro, North Carolina.

And it's growing, says Herb, because his staff is less restricted than his larger competitors and have flexibility in matching or under-cutting competitors' rates quickly without having to consult a superior.

That's one of the reasons a banker in Hungary has approached Discount to open outlets there and there are plans for the company to expand into Austria next year.

"You have to take a risk," says 47-year-old Herb, sitting in his airy office on an industrial estate in Concord.

"But if I were doing it today, I'm not sure I could have made it."

Singer had been working for another car rental firm, Budget, when he and Rhoda sat

Please see SINGER'S/page C6

Discount Car and Truck Rentals

Business: One of Canada's larger car rental companies, with branches in the U.S. and planning to expand into eastern Europe.

Head office: Toronto

Employees: 500

History: Founded in 1980 by Herb Singer and his wife, Rhoda. They entered an already crowded and cutthroat market to take on such household names as Hertz, Tilden, Avis and Budget. Now they have sales of more than $50 million a year.

We were big news when we succeeded.

The successful entrepreneur in the early days – although I never had much time to ride around in a convertible.

I told a buddy who was with me in Brooklyn the first time I saw
Rhoda, "I'm going to marry that girl." I kept my word.

Herb Singer

Jay, Sarah and Barry.

*Here's how I count my wealth and my blessings. Never, ever
underestimate the value and joy of family (and grandchildren are a
bonus beyond measure).*

Forty years and still counting...

Everyone who watches a Blue Jays game is reminded of our name and our business.

Herb Singer

CORPORATE CULTURE

> *Discount has continued identifying new opportunities to expand by looking at the industry and identifying customer needs. Thanks to a culture of employee empowerment, those ideas often come from the employees at every level of the company*

Barry Singer, left, and his father, Herb Singer, Discount founder, stress customer service.

From humble start to national brand

DISCOUNT CAR AND TRUCK RENTALS

By ALEXANDRA LOPEZ-PACHECO

Thirty years ago in Hamilton, Ont., Herb and Rhoda Singer saw a market need for a much stronger level of customer service in the car rental industry — so they launched Discount Car & Truck Rentals to do just that.

The obstacles were formidable. Not only was the country in a recession at the time, the start-up also faced major multi-national competitors. Mr. and Ms. Singer, however, had a clear philosophy that was focused on a symbiotic relationship between the com-

Today, Discount is a nationally-recognized brand with more than 300 locations across Canada and in parts of Australia. The company has been an innovator in the industry. It was the first to focus on the insurance replacement rental car sector.

"Herb actually sat back one day and looked at the industry and he saw that the insurance replacement rental car segment was under-serviced," says Rhoda Singer. "So he began talking to the different insurance companies and dealerships and asking them how it worked. They said it was very ad hoc, and we thought this is a really good area to get into. When you're in an accident, it's really good to go to someone who takes you by the hand and says, 'you know what, let me take you through the pro-

replacement rental business, the company's leisure rental side has also grown significantly. "More people, instead of getting in a plane for a short trip, are renting a car because travelling by air has so many more inconveniences these days," Mr. Singer says.

Others rent cars for weekend trips to avoid penalties for exceeding their lease mileage maximums. And still others prefer to own smaller, more environmentally friendly cars with better gas consumption — and rent larger ones as needed on special occasions. "We want Discount to be your virtual garage with any size car or truck that you need."

In fact, the company has also built a loyal corporate clientele base as well as strong relationships in its commercial truck rental business, especially handling extra trucking needs for companies during high-peak business periods. "We're their safety valve," Mr. Singer says.

One of Discount's competitive advantages in the truck segment has been its commitment to safety and quality — which received validation in 2005 when the Ontario ministry of transportation inspected all fleets in the truck rental industry to see if they

cess that you need."

The company prides itself most on the walk — making it real — and from the beginning its founders were determined to provide employees with the skills and autonomy they need to be empowered with entrepreneurialism. "When someone joins the company at a branch level, there's an intensive training program with checklists along the way, to make sure they're getting all the skills and achieving all the knowledge that is good for their career path with us. Once they reach the six-month evaluation, anyone who qualifies is put into what we call the Circle of Influence, and at that point they go through 12 months of three different four-month modules."

These modules teach the employees nothing less than the A to Z of running a business. "We pride ourselves in that we focus to help them on everything to do with business: relationship building, sales, receivables, accounting, looking after the vehicles," says co-owner Rhoda Singer. "So at the end at least we know, whether they stay with us or go on to other companies, that we have given them the tools to run a business."

Critical to the corporate culture is also the idea that if the company treats its em-

ployees exceptionally, its employees will do the same with customers. "We believe so strongly in rewarding and recognizing our employees. We want to make sure they understand the company and all the different ways they can contribute to its success," Mr. Singer says.

Beyond financial bonuses based on performance, the company conducts team-building lunches and dinners, trips and cruises, pub nights and bowling nights, and it pays for training and education such as MBAs. It also has The Going the Extra Mile Award, which was borne from a recognition that its employees were, in fact, going the extra mile for customers.

"There are so many examples of this," Mr. Singer says. In one case, an employee went after work on a Saturday to help a customer move after all the people who'd signed up to help the family backed out at the last minute. Many will stay after closing hours to wait for a customer who is delayed in picking up the car. "The Extra Mile Award is a way for us to celebrate how

> *We believe so strongly in rewarding our employees*

somebody has really made a difference in one of our customers' life," Mr. Singer says.

The employees play a deciding role in what charities the company supports, which are many, including Mothers Against Drunk Driving, Sick Kids Hospital Foundation, Second Harvest, George Hull Centre and the Chase McEachern Defibrillator Tribute Fund.

"One employee wanted to raise money for the Canadian Breast Cancer Society because a family member had had a scare. So we said, 'OK, let's organize a staff barbecue,'" Ms. Singer says. "Everyone was to give $1 for two hotdogs, a drink and a dessert. Instead, people were putting in $10 or $20 into the box."

pany and its customers.

panies that take advantage of the resources that Discount offers them. As the company's core insurance

been extended to its insurance replacement customers.

Discount was also the first of its kind to embrace sustainability with a formal carbon footprint assessment and plan. "Starting from our energy usage, to our buildings, our carbon footprint, our water usage, our green cleaning products for washing the cars, we decided we needed to make the commitment," Mr. Singer says.

As part of its leading-edge move, Discount purchased Toyota Prius hybrid cars to offer environmentally aware customers that option but also to educate customers who, once aware of the environmental benefits of a hybrid, might prefer it.

"And we were the first company in Canada to come up with vanity numbers, 310-

Rental car company likes to walk the walk

EXTRA MILE AWARD

Employees look to improve customer service

"We really have a culture of empowerment and ownership in our locations, where everyone who works there feels it's their company," says Barry Singer, the company's vice-president.

"Everyone is always thinking on how to improve customer service and the company. So when you have over 2,500 people across an organization thinking along those lines, the ideas filter to the top and they get acted on very quickly because they're happening at a grassroots level."

That's the talk, but the

> *It's nice when the news media recognizes the steps you've taken to reward employees well, provide exceptional customer care, and take steps to raise environmental awareness, as this article in the National Post explained in detail. Of course, it's even better when customers reward you with their business.*

EIGHT

Franchising and Unexpected Opportunities

I'm constantly amazed at the number of people who say things such as, "Maybe I could open a little restaurant on my own," yet they've never boiled an egg in their lives. Or, "I could start a fishing camp up north somewhere, with rental rooms and boats." They say this because they like fishing. They believe that running a business — even a small business — is as much fun as putting a worm on a hook and tossing it in the water. The way I see it, their new business has as much chance of surviving as the worm.

Before launching and running a successful business, you need to know two things as well as you know your own shoe size.

First, you need to learn every aspect of the business you're considering. If you're not a great natural cook, don't rely on somebody else to make you a big success in the restaurant business. And even if you are a great chef, don't think that cooking is all you need to know. You need knowledge of everything that goes on in the restaurant business, from servicing the stoves you'll use to prepare your meals to designing and printing the menus that will sell your dishes to your customers.

Can you learn this on the job? Sure you can. You can learn how to fly a jet plane on the job too, but I won't be one of your passengers.

The other thing you need to know is how business works generally. If I run a car rental business, and you run a restaurant, how much can we have in common? More than you may expect. We'll both have to deal with hiring and firing, setting prices, paying taxes, chasing suppliers, pleasing customers, and a hundred other things. Either you learn it now, or you learn it later. Trouble is, your biggest lesson in running your own business may arrive the day you go broke.

The Middle

Franchising is a middle ground between being an employee and being an independent businessperson. It sets the course and provides the discipline for people who want to be in business for themselves, but don't want to invent a wheel that is already rolling. The franchisor writes the bible containing all the rules, guidelines, and lessons needed to make the business a success and expects the franchisee to follow it.

If you want to start your own car rental business on a national scale, good luck to you. You'll need scads of money to start. But money alone won't get it done. You'll also need systems, promotion, advertising, insurance, location selection, and a dozen other essentials. If you handle all of these on your own, how do you know they work? And how long will it take your customers to get to know and trust your company? Can you survive until they do?

Franchising is designed to help both sides. Franchisees get a proven system and a recognizable name. Franchisors get a source of capital to help them grow and expand. Sounds good, but things aren't always equal, especially in the minds of the franchisees. It often seems that if the franchisee is successful, it's because of their hard work, and if the franchise fails, it's the franchisor's fault.

It's a love/hate kind of business. Both sides need each other, but sometimes — not always — they grow to resent each other. I've had a number of married franchise holders get divorced after building their operations into success. Whenever this happens, and the couple begins to divide their marital assets, things grow complex. Often one ex-spouse can't afford to buy out the other, and now we've got a headache. If the franchise doesn't survive, how do we maintain Discount's presence in that market? Searching for a buyer can be a long drawn-out and costly process. The best solution is for us to take over the franchise ourselves, making it a corporate-owned operation. We've also had to assume franchises to make sure the bank doesn't suffer a loss from a failure and maintain the company's presence and reputation in that market.

From time to time, we have to remind franchisees that they're independent only up to a point. This occurred once when a franchise operator became ill, and his wife decided they could no longer run things. Instead of informing us and letting us deal with the situation, she called the bank and said, in effect, "Come and get the keys to the place — we're out of here." Our normal procedure would have been to assume control of the franchise; make sure the financial obligations were met; keep the employees working; and continue serving customers. The way the wife handled it, we couldn't do a thing. Everybody suffered — except the bank, of course.

Some people lose sight of reality when they make a few bucks and get a little authority. Like the franchisee who, if a customer asked to rent a blue Buick and there wasn't one on the lot, would go out and buy one, even when he had fifty other vehicles sitting around gathering dust.

For reasons like these and others, we've cut back on the number of licence holders in recent years. If a franchisee makes noises about selling their business, we're the first to step up and buy it. As I write this, you can count the number of Discount franchises in Canada on one hand. The rest are corporate-owned and operated.

Selling franchises enabled us to grow and, in the process, enabled many of our licensees to become wealthy. Buying a franchise is still a good alternative for someone who wants to become an almost-independent business person. In our business, we have decided to depend on them less as time goes by.

The Big Dream

I'm all in favour of people launching their own businesses because they believe they have the concept, the energy, and the drive to take their ideas and make them work. And I'm not going to suggest that you, or anyone, should forget about making your dream a reality. I just want to warn you to be cautious at the beginning. Starting a business from scratch has never been easy, and it's getting more difficult with every passing day.

One reason it's becoming more difficult is because of the speed at which things keep changing, especially when technology is involved.

Here's an example: I recently attended a seminar put on by some ambitious guys who were launching a streamlined way of auctioning used cars by telephone. This interested me, because we sell between 100 and 200 cars every week. We want to move those cars quickly at the lowest cost to us, and these guys promised an efficient way of doing things.

They had paved about 100 acres of land near Highway 401, west of Toronto, where the cars were to be gathered and displayed under lights inside security fences. They said they would charge sellers $250 for every car they sold, taking some of the problems off our hands. When I saw the concept and heard the terms, I realized these guys had blown themselves out of the water. Why? Because they underestimated just how fast the world is changing.

I didn't need 100 paved acres of land, and I sure didn't need the hassle of moving our cars to their outdoor showroom. I had just launched a website and made it accessible to all my prime customers, including every used car dealer in the area. Visitors to the site can see what we're offering, examine all the data on each car available, check our price for individual vehicles, and know that every car comes with a guarantee. If the buyer thinks he got a lemon, we'll take the car, and either refund every penny he paid, or let him choose another car from the selection. And I didn't need to spend money on paved lots and big lighting standards. Nor did anybody else in the business. That way of dealing with used cars is past, and these guys, who must have lost millions on their idea, were too slow to spot it.

If you've been mulling over a business idea for a few years and are ready to get it started, make sure it's not already obsolete. Things move fast these days.

I keep hearing about young people, barely out of high school, who are working somewhere in Silicon Valley or Waterloo, Ontario, or a dozen or more places in the world who are busy creating new systems and gizmos that I can't begin to imagine. Not all of these ideas will make the inventors billionaires. But enough will succeed to change every part of our lives, from buying a hat to tying our shoes. We can't see them coming, and we won't know they've arrived until we hear how many millions of dollars the people who launched the companies have made. They're out there, and the first thing that a budding entrepreneur needs to understand is the speed with which the world keeps changing.

When Opportunity Knocks

Many people decide to launch businesses when they've spotted opportunities coming down the road toward them or when they hear opportunities knocking at their doors. That's the fable, anyway. Here's the truth: Real opportunities are not that easy to spot. They disguise themselves as something else. And they drive by your house instead of knocking on your door. You have to get out and look for them.

True story: Back in the early 1980s, a young guy who worked for a computer service company in Toronto was sent by his boss to a major computer show in Las Vegas. The young guy was really excited. He was also driven to succeed. He had never been to a computer show and had never even been to Las Vegas. He was ordered by his boss to walk around the show, look at the displays, get a better feel for the business, maybe pick up some brochures, and report on things when he returned.

When his flight stopped in Detroit, one of the passengers who boarded the plane there sat next to the young guy. The two men began talking and discovered they were both going to the computer show. The older man, whose name was Robert Metcalfe, explained that he was attending the show in search of representatives to sell a program he had invented and patented. He called it Ethernet and told the young man that it enabled personal computers, which were still in their infancy, to talk to each other and exchange data. For example, a dozen computers could talk to the same printer, and the printer would respond by following the PC and its operator's instructions. When Metcalfe explained how Ethernet worked, the young guy from Toronto quickly understood the basic technology. More than that, he saw the opportunity.

This is old hat to us now, but back before the Internet and a load of other things we take for granted were invented, Metcalfe's idea was ground-breaking. Some of the benefits were obvious: Instead of a company buying a separate (and at the time expensive) printer for each desktop computer, one printer could serve a dozen computers. Computers were popping up on desks everywhere, and they all needed printers. Imagine how much money companies could make with this new Ethernet concept. And there were more benefits beyond saving money on printers. Instead of employees carrying files, known back then as floppy disks, from one computer to another, they could send information back and forth with a single keystroke. It was all faster, cheaper, and more accurate — a real breakthrough. Somewhere in the young man's mind were other possibilities — like extending the reach of a fixed number of computers beyond the same office or the same company.

"Do you have representatives in Canada?" the young guy from Toronto asked Metcalfe.

"Not yet," Metcalfe replied. "You interested?"

By the time the plane landed in Las Vegas, the young man had tied up the rights to distribute the program in Canada, scratching out the deal on notepad paper. He got off the plane in Las Vegas, walked directly to the airline counter, and exchanged his return ticket for the next flight back to Toronto, without setting foot inside the computer show.

"Are you nuts?" his boss said when he showed up at work the next morning. "I sent you to the computer show to learn about our business, not buy somebody's dumb idea."

When the young guy tried to explain the opportunities of networking, his boss said, "We don't need networking or whatever it is. We're doing fine servicing computers. We'll keep doing what we've been doing."

The young guy thought for a minute before resigning on the spot. Then he had his agreement with Metcalfe drawn up formally, as he had promised, borrowed money to cover the first year's rights on the program, and went to work.

A few years later the young guy, whose name was Robert Herjavec,[2] had built his company into a leader in network and Internet security. He had seen the explosive potential of networking, and he was able to look ahead and anticipate the day when companies and individuals could do more than send pictures of themselves and their pets over the Net. Eventually the idea that was born with Robert Metcalfe would expand to include transferring money and confidential documents back and forth to each other. When it did, the computer industry would require the electronic equivalent of Brinks trucks to make sure the money and documents got to the right people and stayed out of the hands of crooks. Herjavec built his company on the basis of providing this service ahead of others, and doing it better. In 1999, he sold his company to AT&T for something in excess of $100 million. After a few years of waiting out the non-competitive clause in the sale, he launched yet another company to offer the same service using a revised, more active approach, and he built this new company well beyond the value of his first operation. As I write

---

2   You may recognize him from his role on the panel of CBC-TV's *Dragons'*
     Den and the NBC-TV show *Shark Tank*.

Herb Singer

this, I understand he is expanding into the U.S., Europe, Australia, and beyond.

That's what happens went you keep your eyes open for opportunity. It almost never knocks on your door and invites you to come out and play.

Sometimes it sits next to you on an airplane.

So What?

It's important to acquire as much knowledge about your work and your business relationships as possible. There is no such thing as useless information. You never know where one piece of knowledge connects with another to your advantage. It's obvious — or should be — that you must learn everything about the job you're hired to perform or have chosen to do. It's not as obvious, but almost as important, for you to learn as much as you can about what everybody else in the business or company does and how they do it.

Also: If you are considering launching your own business, don't copy something that others are already doing. Find something that is totally different, or is filling a proven need, or that sets you apart from the rest of the crowd. Herjavec was the first to fill a need that was on the verge of showing itself. I was hardly the first to start a rent-a-car business, but I offered an exclusive feature that appealed to my customer base. That, and about thirty years of hard work, made me the overnight success I am today.

NINE

Be Your Own Hero
(and Choose a Few Others)

Some time ago, one of our corporate-owned branches received a telephone call from a customer who had rented one of our cars and driven it to Tennessee. She explained that she had been involved in an accident. She was unhurt, and the damage to the car was minimal, but as a result of the accident one door wouldn't close properly. The accident had occurred in heavy rain, which was now entering the car through the window, making it difficult to drive. Was there anything we could do back in Canada?

As a matter of fact, there was. Two of our employees hopped into one of our cars, drove it all the way to Tennessee, handed the keys over to the customer and brought the original car back for repairs.

I don't know how much the trip cost us. The amount would be several times more than we charged to rent the car, so it represented a major loss. I don't even know to this day if the accident was her fault.

So what did I do when I heard about their dash south with a second car, spending several times more money than we could ever hope to make from the rental? I congratulated them — they did exactly what I wanted them to do. More than that, they did what the customer had a right to *expect* them to do. (This, by the way, illustrates something I've been preaching for years: You have more rights when you rent a car than you have when you buy one.)

These guys, in their own way, are heroes to me. They didn't save any lives, and they didn't win any medals, but they knew what had to be done. They didn't stand around saying, "Should we? Shouldn't we?" They took the initiative, acted on their own, and did the right thing.

Our people do this kind of thing so often that we decided to celebrate it and them with our *Going The Extra Mile* award. I've lost count of how often we've awarded this to Discount employees, but I can remember many of the things our people did to earn it. Like the guy at one of our offices who discovered one Saturday that a customer rented a van from us to move his family to a new home, only to learn that all the people who were to help him didn't show up that day. What did our employee do? When his workday was over he went to the customer's home, pitched in to move furniture and other goods, and helped get the family settled at their new address. Many others will make a point of staying after hours to wait for a customer who is late picking up his car. Like the guys who drove to Tennessee with a replacement vehicle, they are heroes to me.

One way or another, we all need heroes. None of us is born with an operation's manual hard-wired into our brains. We look around at an early age to find people who appear to know what to do in a given situation, people who get things done. If we are wise, we find a way to show the same kind of attitude in all aspects of our lives.

Earlier, I named Lee Iacocca as someone worth admiring, and he has become a genuine hero to me. From a business standpoint, there have been others for me, most of them coming from the automobile industry. They include people like George Peebles, President of GM Canada, who knew his business well and, just as importantly, knew how to treat his customers well. Maureen Kempston Darkes, who succeeded George to become the first woman president of a major auto manufacturer, had the same qualities. Rhoda might say that Maureen had even more ability than George because she had to overcome the stigma of being a woman at the top of such a big company. She may be right.

Jim O'Connor, Vice President of Ford's North America Marketing Sales and Service until about 2004, was another guy I admired. He had been President of Ford Motor Company of Canada before being named to the Marketing Sales and Service job, so he knew his way around the company and the industry. Through all the years I knew and worked with him, Jimmy never beat around the bush, always doing his best to please you. If he couldn't find a way to get a deal done with you, he would be totally up front about it. "I can't do this, but I can do that," he would say, and he lived up to every word.

One year, we wanted Ford's price on some cube vans to add to our fleet. The price from their fleet sales department looked high, and when I began digging around, I discovered that FedEx Canada was buying the same number of these trucks as we requested, but were getting a bigger discount. Why? Because they were FedEx?

I called Jimmy and asked what was going on. How could FedEx get a better fleet price than Discount for the same number of trucks? Jimmy promised to look into it and did. He called me back and said, "Herb, you're right. Our guys screwed up. You're getting the vans for the same discount."

And he delivered. Later, I heard that the Ford guys with whom I had been dealing and who had quoted a smaller discount to me than to FedEx were upset that I went over their heads. Too bad. It's all about treating your customers fairly and equally.

If you think the kind of openness, honesty, and response that Jimmy O'Connor demonstrated is common at the upper echelons of big business, I have big news for you. It ain't. In fact, Jimmy's record for being a square-shooter was so good that, when Ford was faced with a class-action suit launched by its Canadian dealers, he was called out of retirement to help settle things. The dealers knew Jim would be fair to both sides, and he was. You can't buy that kind of trust; you have to earn it, sometimes over your entire career.

Another guy I admire is Sergio Marchionne, the Canadian who heads Fiat Chrysler worldwide. I've met him a few times and been impressed — not only by his intelligence, but by how good he is at getting things done his way.

Here's one story about him I like: When he was appointed to run Fiat in Italy, Marchionne discovered that the previous CEO, the chairman and all three vice-chairmen, occupied luxury offices in the penthouse of the company's Head Office building and communicated with each other only through their secretaries. They were acting like a bunch of potentates, not like a team responsible for running a global multi-billion-dollar corporation. One of Marchionne's first moves as CEO was to empty the penthouse and take an office on the fourth floor, next to the engineering department, where important decisions are made and important things happen.

I like that attitude. I also like the fact that he prefers wearing sweaters and pants to the office instead of luxury suits, that he listens to classical music while he works, and that he enjoys his life as an automobile executive — sometimes too much.

He wrecked his personal Ferrari 599 GTB a few years ago (Fiat owns Ferrari), but he still enjoys racing sports cars around racetracks rather than playing golf and sipping martinis. The way I see it, if you're going to work hard, why not enjoy the rewards?

Speaking of working hard, and keeping your life in order: Every Friday night, Marchionne flies from Milan to Detroit for Saturday morning meetings with key people at Chrysler. When the meetings are over, he hops over to Toronto and spends Saturday night with his mother. On Sunday, he flies back to Italy, where he is on the job first thing Monday morning, a job that might include visiting other Fiat-owned plants here, there, and around the world. He sleeps more on his airplane than he sleeps in his own home. That's how you run giant companies. You pay a price in time and energy to justify all that you receive from your efforts.

Good Deeds

Somewhere along the way, it's important to do some good beyond running your company well. Our daughter Sarah has this deep belief that anything we do to assist others will produce a reward for ourselves in the future. It's a form of karma, I suppose, and while I've never been much of a religious man, this is one idea I can buy into because, from a management point of view, it seems to work.

It's not that difficult to apply, either. Sometimes the secret is just keeping your eyes and ears open, understanding what is important to you and the rest of the world, and finding a way to join in.

I'm not going to get into the whole debate about global warming and its cause, but it became clear to me some time ago that the less carbon dioxide we spewed into the air the better it would be for everyone. Our business involves producing CO_2 from the vehicles we rent, which we couldn't change. We could, however, cut CO_2 from other places, and we launched a formal program to get it done. We found ways to reduce the energy to heat our buildings and the water we used to wash the cars, using "green" products that made minimum impact on the environment.

We went farther down that road when we began offering Toyota Prius cars to customers as concerned about environmental impact as we were.

Our decision on how we maintain trucks and how long we keep them in service was a little less obvious to customers but equally important to us.

I was really shocked to learn that every year about 50 heavy wheels come loose from trucks racing along highways in Ontario alone.[3] Most do little or no damage but about a half dozen or so strike some innocent motorists on the highway. I don't have to describe what happens when a 200-pound truck wheel rolling at 100 kph hits a car coming in the opposite direction. Every time

---

3   Toronto STAR, December 22, 2011

it occurred someone was killed or terribly injured, and the cause was traced back to older vehicles being poorly maintained.

We agreed to do whatever it took to eliminate the risk of this happening with a rented Discount truck by imposing strict maintenance and inspection standards, and not keeping trucks or vans in our fleet beyond 24 months. It seems to work. When the Province of Ontario began inspecting truck rental fleets in 2005, every one of our vehicles passed with flying colours — green and blue colours, as I recall…

All of the above sounds like bragging, but it's not intended to. I'm proud of these steps to make the world a little cleaner, safer and, who knows, cooler in the long run. But they weren't entirely my idea. They were born by listening to our customers and our staff about the things that matter to them, and finding a way to respond.

That's it. No brilliant ideas, no midnight brain-storming, no consulting with gurus. Just listen closely, decide what to do, and get it done.

What's the big deal?

What's so rare about respect?

I don't believe in being unfair or difficult with anybody in business. You don't have to be back-slapping buddies with your staff or suppliers, but there's no need to pound your desk or yell over the telephone to get things done. You're not at war; you're running a business, usually with people you've known for years. Some of my best business deals have involved laughter and smiles on both sides, and there's nothing wrong with that.

I take the same approach with our employees. We abide by the rule that says, "Why not treat the other guy (or gal) the same way you would like to be treated?"

Sounds good to me, and we do the same thing whether the employee manages an operation or washes cars. We need them both, so we treat them alike.

This is a long way of explaining how, starting in 2010, Discount was named one of Canada's Ten Most Admired Corporate Cultures for three years in a row. We also won the Consumer's Choice Award for Business Excellence over eleven consecutive years.

I have mixed emotions about these awards. Obviously, I'm proud of the recognition and pleased that our employees know they're working for a company considered pretty good in its operations, especially where people are concerned. Yet, I also wonder why other companies can't do the same damn thing. It's not really that difficult. We didn't set winning awards as a corporate objective. We did what we thought was the right thing to do when it comes to dealing with people. Why can't other companies do it? Is respect for employees really that rare these days?

Maybe it is.

Power to the People

Earlier I mentioned that the two biggest assets we have at Discount are our fleet of vehicles and our thousands of employees. Guess which group needs (and deserves) the most service and attention? I'll save you the effort: It's the people.

Not one of our cars would make it onto the road without our people doing their work at a professional level. Nobody does good work because somebody else wants them to; they do good work because *they* want to. Think about that.

The best way to ensure that people do good work is to give them freedom to make decisions. This is still a new idea to a lot of companies who would prefer to hire robots instead of people. Why? Because robots don't think for themselves. That's not a plus in my book. We don't have robots as customers. We have *people* as customers, and while every one of them is different in his or her own way, they all share the same expectation: They want to be listened to, understood, and treated fairly. Have you found a robot who can do that?

Here's another way we rely on our employees:

Every large corporation worth its salt makes charitable donations — or should. Their motive doesn't matter. It can be to generate good P.R., impress their customers, or that old line about "giving back to the community." The biggest challenge they face is deciding on the charity they want to support. No matter how large and profitable a company may be, it cannot support every charity looking for funds. So who plays the deciding role at Discount? Our employees.

Over the years we have supported a range of charities including Mothers Against Drunk Driving (MADD), Sick Kids Hospital Foundation and Second Harvest, among many others. We couldn't have earned the profit to share with these organizations without the efforts of our people, so why shouldn't they have a voice in deciding where the money goes? Makes sense to me.

Employees who are given freedom to do what's best for the customer are empowered. We empower people by saying, "Do your best for the customer, whatever it takes."

This explains our management slogan: *We've Got Your Back*. If employees do what they believe is best for both sides in a given situation, nobody is going to second-guess them. No one will say, "You should have done it by the book."

We don't go "by the book". We go by the customer.

And we don't preach the importance of putting customers first. We don't have to. It comes naturally to people who have the attitude we look for in our staff. Instead of *We've Got Your Back*, we could have quoted Shakespeare, who wrote in *Hamlet*: "To thine own self be true."

That's a little dated compared with *We've Got Your Back*, but it's an important part of making the most of your journey and of yourself.

So What?

The best things we do in life are the things that come naturally to us and that reflect our best values. Choosing those values and sticking with them as an individual, as a life partner, as a parent, and as an employee or business person, is a critical step in life.

None of us is born with these values imprinted in our minds. We learn and acquire them from those around us and, if necessary, from those we view from a distance. It's why we value heroes. They not only do great things; they show us how to get great things done. All we need to do is pay attention.

TEN

Learn to Get Along with Necessary Evils

Suppose you borrow $70 from someone. You know you'll get around to paying it back sometime, so why worry about it? I mean, 70 bucks is still a chunk of cash but not more than almost anybody can handle, right?

What if it's not $70, but $7,000? Or $70,000? When your debt gets that high, you might wonder how much the interest is costing you, what kind of payment schedule you might set up, and how patient the other person will be if you're a little late on the payments, or if you need to borrow more money. And that's just for $70,000. Now let's go bigger: If you owed $7 million, you might find yourself waking in a cold sweat in the middle of the night, thinking "*Yikes — I owe somebody $7 million!*" To a company like ours, that's almost loose change.

Here's what it's like to run a company like Discount: At any given time, my company owes about $70 million to the banks in Canada. I'll spell it out so you can count the zeros: $70,000,000.

Do I ever wake up in a cold sweat at night and realize that the phone could ring and someone at the bank may say to me, "Okay, Herb — we'd like you to pay us back all the money today, maybe tomorrow at the latest?"

Damn right I do.

Which is one reason the banks scare the hell out of me.

I'm not going to be a big-league bank basher here. We need the banks. The business I launched is both capital-intensive and people-intensive, which means it can't function without relying on bank resources. Unfortunately, banks can also become a necessary evil that is either stroking you or kicking you — sometimes simultaneously. That's why I envy people who don't need banks as much as we do. They may not know how lucky they are.

A banker is like someone who offers you an umbrella while the sun is shining and, as soon as the rain starts to fall, asks for it back again. If someone tries to convince you that a bank wants to be your partner in business, take the idea with a grain of salt. Better yet, take it with a whole shaker of salt or maybe two.

They can't be your partner because banks don't think like you. They don't deal with the same business concerns as you, and they certainly don't see the same vision you have for yourself and your company's prospects.

Several years ago, a guy named Frank O'Dea went to his bank for a loan to expand a line of specialty coffee shops. He and his partner had built a good little business from scratch. (This was before the rise of Starbucks.)

Frank's company sold servings of premium coffee, freshly made, at a premium price in an atmosphere where people could relax and savour coffee from beans harvested from all over the world. It was a new concept, and it was catching on. Boy, did it catch on!

O'Dea and his partner had settled all of their obligations to the bank from the beginning. Their credit was Class "A".

One day, they learned that a perfect location for their operation was available at the Eaton Centre in Toronto. It was an opportunity they couldn't afford to pass up, but they would need a loan to finance the new outlet. They wrote a detailed pitch to their bank, outlining what they needed, why they needed it, how they expected to grow and profit from it, and all the other things banks want to hear before they hand over cash. They were confident about getting the money they needed.

The bank manager turned them down flat. O'Dea was shocked. "What's the problem?" he asked.

"You guys already have seven coffee shops," the bank manager said.

O'Dea agreed. They sure did, and all were doing well. The shops, by the way, were called Second Cup.

"We think that's all the specialty coffee shops the business can absorb," the manager said. "You'll likely go broke on this one. There's no room for any more coffee shops selling the stuff at the prices you're asking."

Remember, this was before the arrival of Starbucks, Tim Hortons, Timothy's, and the others. Frank and his partner had been bright enough to recognize the potential growth of premium coffee shops long before anyone else did. They were the first to develop the concept, and they were looking to the future. Their bank manager was thinking…well, I'm not sure what he was thinking. Maybe that a guy like him would never pay more than fifty cents for a cup of coffee, no matter how good it was, and he doubted that anyone else would either.

Within a few years there would be literally a thousand times the number of coffee shops operating across Canada as there had been on the day the bank manager decided Canada had all the premium coffee shops it could handle. The manager may have known a lot about calculating interest rates and payment schedules, but he sure didn't know much about selling high-quality coffee. This didn't stop him from pretending that he did.

For the record, O'Dea and his partner walked out of that bank and down the street where they found a bank manager who could see the bigger picture. This bank manager agreed to the deal, Second Cup changed banks, opened the Eaton Centre location, and launched a series of franchised Second Cup shops. Eventually they built Second Cup into a large and profitable operation, selling the company for a nifty profit.[4] In the process, of course, they made the new bank millions of dollars in fees, because one manager understood things as well as the customers did.

The Trouble with Banks

My experiences with banks haven't been quite as dramatic as O'Dea's, but the general nature of how they operate has affected my way of assessing them. I'm not going to name specific banks in telling my tales of how I deal with them because the stories reflect the decisions of individuals who are no longer employed with the banks and no longer making or following the same policies. Besides, if I get too negative about them, I could be slitting my own throat, figuratively speaking. I suspect every horror story I have to tell about dealing with big banks can be told by almost every other business of our size.

Here are a few anyway: Many years ago, I borrowed $3,000 from a major bank to buy a car. I had stuck with the same bank for forty-five years, building my business by borrowing money at the bank's going rate. I never missed a payment or stiffed the bank for a single dime over all those years. Along the way, Rhoda and I and our team built Discount into one of this country's most successful privately owned businesses.

One day, the bank where I had made that first $3,000 loan many years earlier assigned a new person to handle our account. No big deal, I thought. Everything is laid out in the company's balance sheet. Around the same time, one of our franchisees got into trouble and had to declare bankruptcy. He had been running his own show, as franchisees tend to do, but it turned out he had been running it badly.

He had been dealing with the same bank as we did and had developed a business relationship with them on his own.

---

4   This story is told in detail in O'Dea's book *When All You Have Is Hope* (Viking-Penguin, 2007)

Remember, we're talking two different businesses here. One was Discount, the franchisor. The other was the Discount franchisee, who ran his own operation and made all his own decisions when dealing with the bank.

Didn't matter. The bank, I was told, was concerned about losing money due to the franchisee's financial difficulties, and the banker lumped us — the franchisor — in as part of her evaluation. I called the new person handling our account and said, "Give me the cars and the credit line from the bankrupt franchise, and I'll get you off the hook. I'll assume the franchisee's debt, move the cars for you, and settle everything to the penny."

She wouldn't go along with it.

"Have you reviewed our balance sheet?" I asked, knowing that it would reveal no problems with the way we were running the business.

"Yes," she said, "and we still have a concern."

I suspect she couldn't read a balance sheet correctly. I could almost hear her muttering, "Discount owes $70 million, and one of their licensees owes us money. There's gotta be a catch to this somewhere."

She couldn't see the catch because it didn't exist. But this didn't stop her from thinking that it did. She may have had dreams of uncovering some imaginary problem, perhaps parlaying her discovery into a senior position with the bank's head office. Whatever her motive, she hired a bunch of expert accountants to review everything we did, every dollar we owed, and every asset we had to back it up.

The review found nothing out of order, which is what I expected. The auditors examined the figures and understood that we were using the bank loans exactly as we should.

End of story? Not a chance. The bank charged me $100,000 for the cost of the review, which I did *not* expect. How could I? After more than forty years of loyalty to the bank, during which time my trustworthy company paid tens of millions of dollars in interest and charges, the bank decided to hit me with this new charge.

Isn't that like shooting me in the foot and asking me to pay for the bullet?

The first thing I did was fire my regular accountants and replace them with KPMG. At our first meeting, I gave the new accountants their initial assignment: Go to the bank, explain things to them, and get this settled because it's keeping me awake at night. Show them their mistake and get me back my $100,000.

The new accountants made their pitch, but the bank refused to settle. By this time, our case had been assigned to a special loans manager, a guy who saw himself as some kind of bounty hunter that wouldn't come home without dragging some desperado behind him. There was no desperado. There was no reason to go hunting for one. There was just us, running a growing business that relied on the bank for our substantial borrowing needs and able to service our debt easily.

But it wasn't really about us. It was about one guy who had mismanaged his franchise and went broke and a bank that turned a blind eye to the fact I had offered to cover the franchisee's obligations.

I received no response to my offer to take the franchisee's cars, assume the debt, and settle things. The accountants said they would run this thing down. But, as I kept insisting, there was nothing to run down. And I was proven right. Our dealings with the bank were found to be entirely correct. Not a penny had been misplaced.

By the time they were finished looking for a non-existent needle in a haystack, the bank spent, I understand, $4 million before somebody looked around said, "You know, Singer's right. There's nothing out of place here."

Then they closed their books and went out for a beer. Or something. That's how much they valued my immaculate record going back forty-plus years.

So do not play that tune to me about banks wanting to be my — or your — business partner. I don't buy it.

That experience taught me a lesson, one you can absorb for yourself: Do not trust the person you deal with at a bank to fully understand your operations, your needs, or even your value to the bank. Get to know people at a higher level than your day-to-day contact and ensure that they realize what's going on — the kind of business you run, the way you run it, and the success you are having. Since receiving the $100,000 invoice from the bank, I make it a point to acquaint myself with individuals near the top of every bank I deal with. I have a lunch here, send a letter there, spend a little time schmoozing over there, and eventually I've got a buddy to call when the bank trips over its own feet because somebody at a lower level is trying to make a name for themselves.

Playing by the Rules

I understand that banks need rules. Every organization needs rules, and if your organization's business involves loaning millions of dollars, you *really* need rules in place. It's when the rules override your common sense that you look silly. Like the experience we had recently with a major American bank whose name you would recognize immediately.

We borrowed $30 million from this American bank because their terms were good, and they wanted our business. Everything went well. We used the money as we said we would, and we made payments back to them as we promised. They were so pleased with our business that the bank sent me a debit card, meaning I could withdraw cash from the account any time I wanted.

That's good, I thought, but maybe I should have a VISA credit card from this bank because Rhoda and I often travel in the United States where some places don't take debit cards. So I asked for a VISA card issued by the big American bank.

They turned me down.

Honestly. Said "Sorry, we can't send you a card right away."

"I don't understand," I said to the guy I had dealt with at the bank. "You make $30 million available, you send me a debit card on the account, and you tell me you value me as a good customer. But you won't issue me a VISA card? How do you explain that?"

The VP said that they couldn't send a VISA card until they did a complete credit check on me, which would include a list of every asset I owned and every loan I had ever signed. That was the rule, and they were not prepared to break it. Or even bend it. I could have $30 million for the company I owned, but I couldn't get a credit card to spend three bucks on a bag of potato chips. How sensible is that?

Banks Are Like People

All big banks are alike in some ways and different in others. So they're like people. They have different personalities and different ways of trying to get along with you. I know because over the years I've had dealings with many of the big Canadian banks.

Some of my experiences have been good, and some have not been so good. I avoid dealing with one bank because, frankly, I sense that the top guy is prejudiced. Why should I give my business to someone who has no respect for me?

The banks aren't happy when I and you and a lot of other people criticize them. They tell us, in effect, "You need our money."

Well, not quite true. At a certain point it's *my* money we're talking about. My debt, my security, my reputation for paying my bills, and my loss if things go wrong.

You may read about businesses going broke or being in serious trouble every day of the week. But you have not and, I predict, will *never* hear about any of the big banks in this country going broke. You will almost certainly hear of banks making money year after year. That's not a bad thing, of course. But you have to ask yourself: Who is really taking the risk in the banking business?

The Only Partner for Me

In addition to dealing with banks, sometimes you'll find yourself dealing with a business partner or two. Or three or four. A lot of people in business manage to make partnerships work. Most of them are professionals, including those working in advertising agencies, law firms, medical clinics, and so on. They share expenses, profits and — they hope — long-term success.

In my personal experience, the only partnership that has worked well for me is the one I have with Rhoda, which is more dependent on a marriage licence than on a business contract. In contrast, some of the biggest problems and losses I have encountered over the years involved business partnerships or deals where I had only minority control over things.

I still have a lot of trust in most people. You can't go through life being suspicious of everybody. But I change my policy when it comes to setting up deals with others. My approach has been to avoid any deal where I didn't have 51 percent of the package — in other words, when it comes to the crunch, if I don't have control I'm out of the picture.

This may sound inflexible to some people, but it's a lesson I learned too often to ignore, and I suggest you follow the rule whenever considering a business deal. If they don't give you control, you don't give them the money.

Here's another way to put it: *Even when you trust the dealer, always cut the cards.*

So What?

Dealing with banks is like playing soccer with tigers; you'll run not just to keep the ball moving but also to keep your butt from being bitten.

Don't get me wrong. Banks don't want to crush you. They make too much money from you to do that. But banks are where the money is, and money is power. If someone at a bank decides they don't like you, or can't read your balance sheet, or can't grasp how your business works, you will pay a price and the bank won't pay a penny. And if they do, it's likely to be your penny, not theirs.

*The best strategy is get to know higher-level people at your bank rather than rely on the person assigned to your account. Find someone in a position of authority who understands your business and who understands **you**. Keep their name and number handy and use it when necessary without abusing the relationship.*

It's always better to deal with a buddy than a bank. Always.

Finally: Never become so excited about a business deal that you give up your control of things.

ELEVEN

Family Matters

Everything has a price, including the satisfaction you get out of life. It's not really the price you should worry about. It's the value you place on it and the investment you want to make in it.

I said earlier that you don't have to set the same goal as I set for myself in order to have a fulfilled life. I don't know any teachers, or country doctors, or caregivers who became millionaires, but I admire the ones who are exceptionally good at any of those jobs. And if that's the goal they set for themselves, they have my thanks and congratulations.

Not everyone wants to be, or can be, a doctor or a teacher. Many people want more material reward from life. They will find satisfaction only by finally listening to the inner voice that says, "When are you going to get off your keister and prove to the world/your spouse/your mother/yourself that you can be a success and make lots of money?"

If you're driven enough to heed that nagging voice, then maybe you should do what it suggests. But do it realistically. Recognize that the world changes almost daily. What's more, the rate of change is speeding up. Ideas that sound good today are old-fashioned tomorrow, and by the time you spot a bandwagon coming down the road and try to hop aboard, it's already crowded with people punching and kicking each other to make more room for themselves.

I'm not trying to dissuade you from setting out on your own. I still think it's better to try and fail than never to try at all. But understand one thing: As the speed of change increases, so does the cost of being in the race. And I'm not just talking about the entry fee. The higher the goal, the more you'll need to pay for the entire journey.

How much will you have to pay? Remember that old cliché, "If you have to ask the price, you can't afford it."

If you have to wonder if it's worth it to successfully fulfil your dream, maybe you had better forget about it.

Many people want to achieve success on a grand scale and expect to live something called "a balanced life". They assume they will have all the time and energy they need to spend with their families and their friends while running their businesses.

Here's the bitter truth: You can't have both.

When Rhoda and I were building Discount from scratch, we didn't know what life was outside the business. Earlier, I said that our eldest son wasn't sure he had a father for the first five years of his life. I'm not exaggerating. I had to find ways to assure him that the stranger he encountered in his house from time to time really was his mother's husband.

The people who operate Discount licensed branches take the same approach.

As it turns out, all are men, and their wives are either fully involved in running things, as Rhoda was, or not involved at all.

Now, About the Children...

When both the business and our children were mature, Rhoda and I had to make a decision about the involvement of our sons, Barry and Jay, and our daughter, Sarah, in Discount. Our first rule was that they would play a role in the company only if they wanted to. We'd heard too many stories about parents trying to force their sons and daughters into careers that didn't interest them.

Sometimes it was taking over the family business. Sometimes it was becoming a lawyer or a doctor or some other profession that the parents would like to be able to brag about. And sometimes the offspring who had made his or her parents so proud as a toddler drifted into other things that the parents were not so pleased about. If this happens to you, there is no point becoming a tyrant and forcing your child to join you in the family business.

If you've raised your children to think for themselves, it is a mistake to try to run their lives. It's also a great way to alienate your offspring.

Another concern that Rhoda and I shared involved the role each would play in the business, if they chose to be a part of it. We decided each would assume the position in the company that suited their skills and interests, more than their sequence of birth. Seniority might be appropriate for trade unions, but not for our family.

Rhoda and I also emphasized the importance of education. If our sons and daughter wanted to be in the business, they had to acquire an MBA. An MBA doesn't transform anybody into a business genius on its own, but it's a great way to acclimatize them to the decision-making process. It's also a pretty good way to instil discipline and attitude when it comes to setting goals and achieving them. All three of our kids have MBA degrees.

Finally, even with the family connection and an MBA after their name, none of our children could work for Discount until they had worked at least two years for a different company to acquire a range of experience in dealing with other businesses, other systems, other kinds of people.

Our sons, Jay and Barry, got their feet wet at Discount smack in the middle of the 2007-2008 recession and all of its uncertainty and financial upheaval. Nothing could have prepared them for the kinds of challenges they had to face, including their MBA studies.

"*This* is the MBA," Jay said in the middle of the turmoil. When it comes to gaining practical experience, he was totally correct.

Jay and Barry work hard and are good at their jobs. I know you're thinking, "Herb's saying that because they're his kids," but trust me on this — it's true. They do their jobs well and still get home in the evening to have dinner with their families and take the kids camping or wherever on weekends.

The history of family-run businesses is littered with the wreckage of companies whose succession plans fell apart for various reasons. I get the sense that a lot of parents who have built a family business handle the process of passing it on by saying either, "There it is, good luck, we're off to Florida," or "You better do this our way because we'll be looking over your shoulder, and if you screw up, you're gone!"

Neither way is good.

Rhoda and I have a terrific relationship with Jay, Barry, and Sarah, yet I felt that we all needed to know as much as possible about the process of passing a company from one generation to another. So we invested in a consultant who suggested how to make it work, how to run family meetings, how to communicate among the family, what kinds of crises to expect, and how to deal with them. We listened, we learned, and we applied the acquired wisdom. It was money well spent.

Things are rolling along well. Jay, who's interested in overall management, is President. Barry, who is a whiz at financial, legal, and governance issues, handles these critically important duties as Vice-President. I come in to the office a couple of days a week, but I intentionally avoid stepping on anyone's toes. I think we've done the succession thing right.

Legacy

Here's something that pleases me immensely: I mentioned that anybody who starts a company that becomes as large and complex as Discount had better forget about living a balanced life where he or she can count on having regular vacations, eating dinner with the family, and making the most of their kids' soccer games.

Rhoda and I missed that. Our children won't. Why? Because it's easier to push a wagon that's already rolling than a wagon that's standing still.

We both worked very hard for many years and missed the chances to play with our kids. Instead, we gave our kids the opportunity to play with our grandchildren. That's the kind of sacrifices you make when you're taking the long view of things.

It took time — years and years — to get our business rolling. When we began to hand it to over the children, the company had momentum. It still needed attention, care, and direction, and always will, but these things can be done without the people at the top committing twelve or fifteen hours to it for 365 days of the year.

This means our grandchildren will thrive with the attention they'll get from their parents — both of their parents. If you're a grandparent, or know how much pride we have in our grandchildren, you'll understand how pleased this makes us feel.

Gold Watches

Speaking of being a grandparent, we don't have a retirement policy at Discount. When you hit 55, 60, or 65 years of age, nobody in the company is going to hand you a gold watch and escort you out the door. If you want to keep working at your job and you can do it well, it's up to you when to retire; it's not up to us.

I'm proud of that policy. I'm not sure it's unique, but I know it's unusual these days. Some companies today say, "Okay, you're 60 years old, congratulations, nice knowing you, and here's your hat."

Then they replace you with two 30-year-olds who, together, are paid less money than the company had been paying you, the new retiree.

If you're the person they're shuffling out the back door while the two 30-year-olds are coming in the front door, what are you going to do now, assuming your health is good? It's a little late, at age 60 or 65, to start saving for your retirement. This is the time when you should start doing other things, like travelling with your partner or pursuing a hobby. You can't do that if you've been living from paycheque to paycheque all your working years. If you didn't start planning things years ago, you will likely be pouring coffee at Tim Hortons just to pay the bills.

There was a time, believe it or not, when many people believed they had a job for life and, when their working years were over, they would have a pension income that let them live out their years in comfort and security. If you're under 30 years of age, this may sound like a fairy tale. But it's true. Companies like IBM, Procter & Gamble, General Motors and most of the other big manufacturing companies almost never fired anybody. Those companies, most people believed, would exist forever. Some are still around, but many are long gone, and most of the companies that are still around trust their employees to look after themselves when it comes to saving for retirement. "Saving for retirement"? Big surprise: A lot of people haven't saved a dime for their retirement.

I'm constantly amazed that people not only fail to plan for the day they are no longer employed, but face their retirement while carrying a mortgage and a lot of debt, including high balances on their credit cards. Too many people these days don't own their credit cards; *their credit cards own them.* If you're maintaining big balances on your credit cards and you're considering retirement, those debts need to be paid now. The banks that issue them have their hands in your pocket, and they will demand that you settle your debts with them.

By the way, do you know the annual interest you pay on your credit card balance? It's probably 20 percent. It may be higher, it could be lower, but that's the standard rate today. Now think about this: If you deposit $1,000 into a bank savings account, the bank will pay you maybe 2 percent a year, which means that after twelve months your money will have earned a whole twenty bucks — which, by the way, is fully taxable, so maybe you'll get to keep half of it. That's the way things work; the banks charge you 20 percent on the money you owe them, and pay you 2 percent on the money they owe you. Now do you see how banks get rich?

I know it's easy to slap down a credit card every time you get the urge to buy something. If you've got a good job and a lot of years of employment ahead of you, why not? You'll pay it off some day.

The trouble is, *some day* comes sooner than you think. And no job is ever guaranteed for life, no matter how good your employer is and how hard you work. Or, as a friend of mine in the financial business once said, "Profits are temporary. Debt is forever."

So What?

Everybody should chase their dream, but everybody should also know the price they will have to pay to catch it. If your dream includes a family life with lots of time to spend with your kids and socializing with friends, forget about becoming a big success by launching a business. If you go ahead anyway, be sure your family — or at least your life partner — shares your dream because they'll be paying for it along with you.

Whether or not you choose the entrepreneurial route, look beyond where you are now to where you'll be a year from now, all the way to your 50s and 60s. You may not be able to see that far from here, but that's all the more reason to plan for it now. Here's how:

- *Minimize your debt, especially your credit cards. Pay them off as quickly as you can.*
- *Get into the habit of paying with cash whenever possible.*
- *Satisfy your needs, not your wants.*
- *Enjoy the best of your financial situation and prepare for the worst.*

- *Discover the joy of having the banks owe you money instead of the other way around.*
- *Accept the fact that your trip through life is a shorter journey than you think.*

TWELVE

Never Underestimate the Value of Laughter

The way I see it, work is serious but life shouldn't be — at least not all the time. Every day of my life, I look for something to make me smile and, if I'm lucky, laugh out loud.

Maybe "look" isn't the best word. I don't go around the office or my home lifting cushions to find a line from Groucho Marx under them. Often the laugh, or the chuckle, or the reason to smile, finds *me*. I just have to be prepared for it.

Here's my point: If you're not enjoying your life, you're doing something wrong. And if you *are* enjoying your life, you have a reason to smile or laugh, preferably in the company of someone you like, at least once a day.

After all the years that Rhoda and I put into building our company, we figure we've earned the chance to treat ourselves, and we do. Not with heavy doses of luxury, believe it or not. But with simple pleasures. Even some that make us laugh.

For example, we like going to Florida in the winter, but we don't have a house there. We have an RV instead. We think it's better than a house in Florida and a darn sight cheaper, too. If we're tired of the town we're in, we drive off to another, usually looking for the best view of a sunset.

Back in Toronto, I drive a Mazda. Why not? Who needs to wheel a car as big as our kitchen through Toronto traffic? Why should I spend $100,000 on a car I hope will impress the guy next to me on the Don Valley Parkway, a road that is like a slow-drifting parking lot half the time? Neither of us is going to move faster whether we're behind the wheel of a Mercedes or a Mazda.

I don't begrudge anybody who spends a pot full of money on a car. Hey, at Discount, we rent BMWs. They're a lot of fun to drive, and I hear they really attract attention from people who know their cars. We love to rent them, but owning and driving one is not my style. I like to keep things simple. And that's difficult. Sometimes you have to force yourself to avoid making things more complicated than they need to be.

Like, you only need one wristwatch. If you own one good watch, you always know what time it is. If you own two watches, you're never sure.

Just Smile

When it comes to fun, I get most of mine by making Rhoda smile, usually by imitating some actor or comedian. Sometimes she laughs so hard at me that she gets hysterical. At times like that, she thinks I'm the funniest guy in the world or at least the funniest guy she knows. I'll tell you: There are a lot of downsides to getting older, but there is a lot of joy out of having fun with a partner you've been married to for 48 years and counting. All the challenges Rhoda and I have faced, all the disappointments and heartaches we have endured, and the achievements we have shared, they make the laughs even more enjoyable.

Rhoda gets a lot of pleasure from our grandchildren, which is another benefit from getting older. You appreciate your kids when you're in your 30s, but you'll never appreciate them more than your grandchildren when you're in your 60s.

Like I said, it's the simple pleasures that count. Next to laughing at my jokes (Maybe they're not that great, but who am I to disagree with a woman as smart as Rhoda?) and being with our nine grandchildren, Rhoda's biggest pleasure these days is to curl up with a good book or sit by the window and do her knitting.

Let me tell you: When you get to a point in your journey where the simple pleasures, the company of friends and family, and the quiet moments to yourself become among the most pleasurable, you have not dropped out of life. You have *discovered* life.

Everybody Puts on Their Pants

I have enjoyed the company of a lot of people I've met in business. Many of them have been big names in finance, investment, insurance, government, and other places. Just mentioning their names can either impress or intimidate some people.

I can be impressed by people, but I'm never intimidated by them, even when they're important to my business. How do I keep from being in awe of them? I use one of the oldest tricks in the book; I remind myself that they put on and take off their pants the same way I do.

When you're not in awe of people, it's much easier to become friends with them because you're comfortable around them. I like hanging out with people who are comfortable to be around. I especially like working with that kind of person. Many of them became more than business associates. They became friends.

I like surprising friends as well. I became a close friend with Jim O'Connor at Ford Canada. I'd call him up every now and then and say, "Let's go have lunch."

Lunch was always a good pastrami sandwich, which he loved. When Jim was in hospital undergoing surgery, I sent him a platter of pastrami, smoked meat, chopped liver, double rye, Kosher pickles — the whole bit. You may have heard people complain about hospital food, but you wouldn't have heard complaints from Jim's room when the pastrami arrived. Which, by the way, he shared with the chairman of the board of the company — both were in the same hospital, at the same time, having surgery.

"Jim," the chairman said when he saw the spread that O'Connor had, "how come you get all the good food?"

Another time, I figured it was time I met the man who headed Royal Bank's property and car insurance division. We were doing a lot of business together, and I figured the better we knew each other, the smoother our business would go. So I called his office one day and suggested we get together for coffee or for lunch, just for a talk.

He wasn't impressed, couldn't find the time. He dealt with a dozen vehicle rental companies. He probably thought, "What's he need to talk to me for?" It took a while to talk him into seeing me. He was busy this time, out of town the next time, in a meeting another time, but I kept at him.

We finally met, and I discover he had survived the Holocaust in Poland. After the war he moved to Mexico, got his Master's Degree at Berkeley, and he and his wife adopted a couple of Mexican Indian kids. He was a very bright guy who could handle a lot of responsibility. Before going to Royal Bank, he had managed a billion-dollar portfolio of investments in South America for the Chase Manhattan Bank.

Between him being in Mexico and me going to Brazil, plus other things, we discovered we had similar pasts — similar enough that we always found something to talk about and something each of us could relate to.

Over the next few years, we went places together because we enjoyed each other's company so much. We went to Israel, where I bought him a prayer shawl; I took him to Brazil and showed him Rio; and we went to Poland where, when he found the house that he had lived in as a small boy, he cried like a baby. When he died a few years ago, his wife asked me to say the prayer at his funeral, and I was honoured.

Ever since our first lunch together, our meetings had nothing to do with business. I wasn't friends with him in hopes of getting more of his business than my competitors. All through the time we knew each other, he split his business fifty-fifty; we got half and the other guys got half. He never favoured me, by giving me more of his business than the next guy, just because we were friends. I would never have thought to ask him for more than we already had or more than we deserved. It would have marred our friendship. I admired him for not offering it, and he admired me for not asking. Why? Because, believe it or not, some things are worth more than money.

Like good friends. Really good friends. You might want to keep that in mind.

So What?

Somewhere in the middle of all the hard work and planning that may occupy your life, you have to find ways to enjoy it. Life isn't easy all the time. I don't think it was meant to be easy. But along the way, I believe we are meant to have fun, to be able to laugh and, more importantly, to make others laugh and feel good about themselves.

One of the best ways to do this is through friendships. Not the kind that you rack up in business, but the kind that make you feel good just to be around people you know and like. You don't need hundreds of friends, like the ones some people brag about on Facebook and elsewhere. If you go through life with a half-dozen good friends, the kind of people who would go into the jungle with you if you asked, you are a lucky person.

And anyone who uses his friends only to further their own interests is a damn fool.

Just thought I'd mention that.

THIRTEEN

Keep Your Road Map Handy

I'm a big fan of Barbra Streisand. We're both from the same generation, which explains some things. But anybody who has heard her sing or has seen her act in movies will agree that the woman has huge amounts of talent.

Listening to her recordings and watching her movies is fine, but there is nothing like seeing and hearing someone like Streisand in person. Through most of my life, when I was busy building Discount into a successful company, I kept telling myself, "Herb, some day you have to go and see Streisand in a live concert."

In October 2012, when the business was running well, and my sons, Jay and Barry, were assuming more responsibility, I heard that Barbra Streisand would be appearing in Montreal. This, I decided, was my chance. Considering her age and my age, I might never get another one. The tickets weren't cheap, and I would have to get to Montreal, but the seats were good and the concert was terrific. The woman could sing as well as ever, and she sure knew how to put on a show.

To me, the most memorable part of the concert wasn't Streisand's singing or the other acts that appeared with her. It was a story she told just before she sang a medley of songs by Marvin Hamlisch, who wrote the Broadway musical *A Chorus Line,* composed the music for *The Way We Were,* and created a lot of other great songs. The guy was brilliant — he won Oscars, Pulitzers, Emmys, and practically every other award for musical talent.

Streisand is a tough cookie, but she came close to tears when she talked about her friend Hamlisch, who had been ill for some time. She told us that she had been meaning to call him for several days, but something always came up and she put it off over and over. Finally, just before going to bed one night, she wrote herself a note: *Call Marvin in the morning.* The next morning, when she finally called, she learned Hamlisch had died just a few days earlier. The lesson, she suggested, was to reach out to those we love and enjoy every day of our life to the limit.

It wasn't very original. You can read this kind of stuff in advice columns in newspapers all over the world. But when someone like Streisand expresses it in front of 30,000 people, it carries weight. It made me realize that we spend the first third of our lives trying to decide who we are, the middle third of our lives being whoever we actually become, and the last third of our lives trying to figure out what the hell happened to the first two-thirds. Where did they go? What did I learn? And what do I do now?

When planning life's journey, we naturally tend to focus on the middle part. What kind of career will we have? What will our ethics be? What goals will we have? How will our family fit in? How much sacrifice are we prepared to make while reaching our goals? How can we make sure that we — and our family — are financially secure?

Most of our focus on the last third of our lives is — or should be — to face those years free of debt, prepared to enjoy life to the fullest. I suggest you also look ahead and recognize the changes you'll be making around the age of 60 or so. Some of them you won't necessarily like. Others will come naturally.

The ones that come naturally will include the realization that so many of the things you spent the early parts of your life accumulating just don't matter anymore. Discarding much of it brings you something precious and often surprising: Freedom.

Sometimes we have to rely on other people to teach us things like valuing the friendships we have and the love of family. We take them for granted, which is easy to do, but we shouldn't do it.

I went all the way to Montreal to hear Streisand sing, and I'm glad I did. I fulfilled a goal I had had for years, and it was worth every penny. I came home with the memory of Streisand's sorrow at not calling her friend until it was too late, and it was a lesson to me.

Now I'm handing it over. If someone who matters deeply to you would benefit from a few kind words, an assurance from you that you haven't forgotten about them, maybe a little encouragement, and if you've been putting it off for a long time, stop procrastinating. Call them now. Put this book down, and go to the telephone.

I'll wait.

Sweat Equity

One of the most difficult balancing acts you need to learn and perform concerns (Surprise!) money. It's fine to work hard and build enough wealth to provide yourself and your family with financial security. But how do you do it…how much do you build up…and what do you do with it?

Rhoda and I built our success by launching our own business and for several years we dedicated much of our waking hours to building its size and value. Not everyone can, or should, even try to do this; as I've said many times so far, it's more important to set your own goals and work toward them, than to prove you can do the same thing with your life as someone else.

The most important reason to accumulate wealth is the one I mentioned above: To build financial security for yourself and your family. Believe it or not, you are unlikely to live forever and you won't be able — or even want — to keep working every day of your life. When you finally stop working, you'll still likely want to eat well, sleep in a comfortable place with a roof over your head, and enjoy certain pleasures like offer gifts to your children and grandchildren, and even take a vacation. That's what retirement is supposed to be about.

Yet most people either refuse to look ahead to that period in their lives, or they assume that someone or something will be around to provide the money they'll need. The "something" is usually the government, in the form of money from the Canada Pension Plan and Old Age Security payments. As I write this, a single Canadian age 65 is eligible for about $12,000 per year from both of those sources. That's it. Are you prepared to survive on $1,000 a month? Will you be taking any vacations to Hawaii or eating many steak dinners with that kind of income?

Your parents — or grandparents — would have relied on a pension plan from their employer to provide at least an adequate income. They might also have relied on somebody delivering milk in a horse-drawn wagon. Neither is very common these days.

Like it or not, we all have to take responsibility for tomorrow by saving and investing some of the money we're earning today. I know it's tough to set aside money that you don't expect to see or use again for ten, twenty, or thirty years from now. But it may not be as difficult as you think.

Most people have no idea how much money they spend on things they don't need, and they are surprised to discover that they can set aside 10 per cent of their income without missing it very much, if at all. In fact, it's possible to save 10 per cent and make it cost half that much. Is there a trick to it? Yes. It's called an RRSP.

If you earn enough money to be in that 50 percent marginal tax bracket — meaning you pay half of every dollar you earn as income tax — you can do the trick. Here's how: Before the RRSP deadline arrives, at the end of February, visit your friendly (sic) neighbourhood bank or credit union and borrow the equivalent of 10 percent of your taxable income in a loan to be paid back in one year. Place all of the money in an RRSP at that same institution. Banks love people saving money for the future, and will give you their very best loan rate. The amount you contribute to your RRSP qualifies you for a tax refund. At a 50 per cent marginal tax rate, this will equal half the amount of money you borrowed. When your tax refund arrives, trot down to your bank or credit union and apply it to the loan. Now you have 100 per cent of your loan in your RRSP, but it cost you only 50 per cent of the total. (I'm simplifying things a little here, but the general rule applies).

There may be a bit of pain associated with applying the tax return cheque to your RRSP loan, but the pain eventually goes away after a few years of doing this when your RRSP statement reveals an impressive pot of money set aside and growing, year by year, without the government seizing a portion of it as taxable income.

It's also far more practical and realistic than the expectation of 11 percent of Canadians — that's more than one out of every ten of us — who, according to a research study conducted by the CIBC just a few years ago, claimed that they did not need any RRSP or pension or anything else to provide retirement income because they expected to win a lottery. I can only assume that they also expect to meet Elvis at Walmart some day...

Whichever way you set aside money for your future, don't make the mistake of placing all of it in a savings account.

Now that you have accumulated a nest egg, you will need to help it grow, and these days bank savings accounts pay barely 1 percent a year, and that's lower than the rate of inflation. Savings accounts these days are where money goes to die, not grow. You shouldn't just be saving; you should be investing.

Say the word "investing" aloud to many Canadians and they think you are speaking a foreign language. Canadians don't invest; they *save*. The truth is that we would be better off if more of us knew how to invest the money we are setting aside for our futures.

The idea of investing frightens people who believe it is complicated. Well, it is. And it isn't. It's like hockey.

Like most sports, hockey can be complicated to learn and play. It can also be simple and fun. It all depends on how involved you want to get in the game, and how involved you *should* get. Sidney Crosby's involvement in hockey is complex because he is constantly studying everything that's happening when he's both on and off the ice. He understands all the tricks — the Neutral Zone Traps, Headmanning the Puck, the Dump-and-Chase Strategy, and a dozen other tactics[5] – and he knows how to execute them and when to use them.

You don't need to know all this stuff to appreciate the game. If you know that it's played on ice with six players per side, that one of the players remains in or at the goal, and that the point is to put a rubber puck in the other team's net as often as possible during a game that consists of three 20-minute periods, you're on your way. Lace up your skates. Grab a stick. Pump your legs, You're on your way.

Investing is similar. Here's what you need to know to get started:

Stocks consist of shares in companies; the price of shares in a company depends on how badly other people want to own them; companies share their profits with payments to shareholders; shares in companies can be combined into groups to create mutual funds; bonds are loans made by you to companies or governments, paid back with interest over periods ranging from one to thirty years; and a combination of shares and guaranteed bonds provides both growth (the price of company shares should rise and dividends should build up over the years) and security (guaranteed bonds will always have a value).

Of course, there's more to learn , but even this limited information is news to many Canadians. Just remember that a little knowledge can be a dangerous thing. Even when you believe you know all the details of investing, it's not wise to start trading in stocks as though they are baseball cards. Your savings for retirement should reflect a conservative approach, and the closer you get to retirement, the more conservative you should become.

In essence, you need a financial advisor to guide you when making investment decisions. Whole books have been written on

---

5   I admit that I had to look these up myself.

investments and advisors. They're probably worth reading, but here are some guidelines that I've picked up over the years.

Advisors make money two ways: From commissions on the stocks, bonds, and other things they trade for you, and from flat fees that are usually a percentage of your investment portfolio. Advisors are salespeople — the more they sell you, the more money they make. Your goal is to maximize the money *you* make, not the money *they* make. That's why you should ask about fees.

Almost all advisors with companies owned by the big banks make their income from sales commissions. They are also instructed on the products to push to their clients. This, of course, makes your interests secondary to theirs. The ones who charge a low flat fee based on the size of your investment portfolio can only increase their income when they increase the value of your portfolio. So remember to ask yourself who will make the most money from any investment — you or your advisor.

Here are other things to keep in mind:

- Your best investment advice, in my opinion, will come from advisors from smaller firms that are dedicated to client service and who can explain their approach. Advisors from these firms depend on fees for performance, not hidden commissions. It may hurt to pay a fee for the advice you get, but in almost every case, the fee will be no lower — and sometimes much less — than the hidden commissions you pay but never see.

- Never invest in something you do not understand. If your advisor cannot explain a proposal to you that makes sense, pass on the idea. If the advisor does this often enough, pass on the advisor.

- When making a decision to invest your hard-earned money, either on your own or with an advisor, do not become greedy. Yes, it's reasonable (but these days difficult) to earn a clear 10 percent growth each year on your investments. It's possible to make 20 percent a year with luck and attention. But forget about anything or anyone who tells you that your portfolio can rise by 50 percent a year without any risk. That's just being greedy and foolish. There is always risk. The secret is to balance the risk with the reward. Buying shares in banks — remember all the money they make — delivers a reasonable reward at a low risk. Things can get really skewed if you don't pay attention. Buying shares in a Peruvian gold mine on the recommendation of your brother-in-law brings high risk and dubious rewards.

- Two things to remember when investing: *If it sounds too good to be true, it probably is.* And: *Pigs get fat. Hogs get slaughtered.*

Lifestyles for Life Stages

When our children were lively and growing, and the company was prospering sufficiently, Rhoda and I bought a large house.

Our previous house had been fine for a family of five. Not large, not ostentatious, but comfortable.

We were attracted to the bigger house because it was frankly a bargain. It had been built by a developer for his own family. The developer, as often happens, had run into financial difficulty and offered us the house at a bargain price, so we bought it.

Listen, it was a fine house. I was proud to be in it and proud to see my family enjoy it in so many ways. We had a dining room that seated twenty-four people and a special room for dancing. The house was so large that, for years, I kept discovering rooms I hadn't known about.

The big house was great when the kids were home at least part of the time. But as time passed they had their own lives to live, their own families to raise, and their own homes to acquire and maintain. In time, the house became too much for Rhoda and me.

When I reached my 60s, and we decided to hand over the operations of Discount to our children, Rhoda and I decided we didn't need the big house anymore. We sold it and moved into a condominium that's maybe a third as big. Most of our furnishings couldn't fit in the condo, so we gave them away — truckloads of stuff we once treasured, but now felt we didn't need. Others could use them.

Did we mourn the loss of all this stuff we had accumulated, stuff that once had defined us? Not a bit. We were free of it. Listen: When you get past 50, and you have good health and freedom, you're more than halfway to happiness. You don't need "stuff".

As I said earlier: When planning your life's journey in your 20s and 30s, accept that the trip will involve stopping to acquire things you feel you need — fashionable clothes, an impressive house, jewellery, maybe boats and motorcycles, and other material goods. If you can get 'em without diving into debt, good for you. Enjoy them. Have fun. They're your reward. They're just not your life…or shouldn't be.

The danger comes when you don't own these things as much as they own you. If your life is dictated more by acquiring, keeping, and using material things than by nurturing your family and friends, something is out of whack. The older you get, the more you will recognize this, and the easier it will be to let go of much of the material wealth you gathered, because you will have realized that you acquired these things not to improve your life, but to keep score of your achievements. And you're keeping score not for yourself but for others around you. Eventually most of us learn to love people, not things, and to admit to ourselves that we can't take it with us.

Or, to put it another way:

He who dies with the most toys wins.

He who dies with the most money loses.

The "R" Word

One of the things most Canadians need to acquire is the means to live a full and comfortable life when they are no longer employed full-time. You know — all those so-called "Golden Years" we intend to enjoy.

There was a time when "retirement" was a positive step forward in life — maybe not like winning the lottery, but attractive on its own merit. Many people fantasized about retirement. No early rising in the morning. No commuting. No snarly boss and co-workers. No worries about being fired.

Time passes. Now the idea of retirement frightens people. Having enough retirement savings on hand is one concern, but even when their RRSPs and TFSAs and home values are bursting with value, "retirement" can still be a scary proposition.

I've done a lot of thinking and a little research that helped me face the prospect of retirement. I boiled everything down to three ideas:

1. **Visualize your life in retirement.** Instead of waiting until you're standing on the street with a gold watch in your hand (*Do they still hand those things out?*) with nowhere to go and nothing to do, spend some time imagining what you would most like to do when retired. Start a new career? Work part-time at your present job with colleagues whose company you enjoy? Travel to places you've always wanted to visit? Build a boat? Ride an elephant? Write a book? Choose the ones that appeal to you most, then start making plans to do them, which will make the transition easier.

2. **Eliminate your debts.** I've already warned about the high interest rates that the banks charge on credit card debt. The problem becomes bigger when you're retired and living on a fixed income. Start your retirement

without owing a penny more than necessary, and you'll face the future with much more comfort and security.

3. **Live within your means.** This was always important during your working years, and it's even more important when you retire. If you always wanted a yacht or a fleet of sports cars, your retirement is probably not the time to acquire them. Your earning power is limited, and your eye should be on conserving enough of your assets to ensure — if I may be so blunt — that they're still hanging around at least as long as you are. Besides — by this point in your life, you should recognize that toys rarely make you as happy as you expect them to do.

Regrets, I Have a Few

Even when you're letting go of material things you have accumulated in your life, you may be gathering other stuff that has built up in your memory. Like regrets.

We all have regrets of some kind. Life, after all, is full of decisions, and not all of the decisions we make prove to be the right ones. Some of us can be happy if just 51 per cent of our decisions prove to be correct.

When you reach your 60s, a lot of the choices you made in your life are seen in a new perspective; one that's clear from all the dust and distractions that were hanging around when you made them years ago. You can't do much at this stage.

They were lessons you learned along the way or hope you did.

So what are my regrets?

On the business side, I wish I had exerted more financial control over people who were in a position to cost me money and headaches. Especially headaches. I don't want to sound untrusting, because I don't believe I am. I don't want to add up all the money it cost me when I put too much trust in too many people who didn't deserve it because it may depress me. And I don't want to change my approach to dealing with people because much of it is based on enjoying their friendship at least as much as I enjoy their business.

The challenge would be maintaining a balance between trust and control. That's not an easy thing to do. But who said anything in life would be easy?

Anyway, that's my biggest regret. Hey, it could be worse.

When I was writing this book, I asked Rhoda if she had any regrets. She told me she had one. She wished she had been able to attend university when she was young. Not just attend, but work at achieving a PhD, maybe in anthropology. She is convinced that she had the drive and intelligence to do it.

Dr Rhoda Singer.

It has a nice ring to it.

So What?

There is an old German, or maybe Yiddish, saying that goes, "We get too soon old and too late smart."

It's true. One of life's great ironies is built on the fact that we never get all the knowledge we need until we're too old to use it effectively. The best thing we can do when we're young — "young" in this case being less than 50 years old — is to listen carefully to someone old enough to have acquired the stuff we have yet to learn.

I'll bet I qualify to be that mentor for most of you. So pay attention.

Have I ever lied to you before?

FOURTEEN
Your Personal Peace Process

I've seen it happen — two people get married, launch their careers, raise a family, enjoy their success and the success of their kids, slide into their retirement years, and congratulate themselves on having had a good life and a great family. Then all hell breaks loose after they pass on.

The same sweet kids, who got along when their parents were alive, turn into suspicious insurgents, each complaining that they have been treated unfairly, unethically, unjustly, and unreasonably — and a lot of other "uns" to go with it.

Sometimes this unrest produces chilly temperatures, like a cold front that moves down from Baffin Island and settles over the family forever. It's like two brothers I knew who lived just a few kilometres from each other and did not speak for almost forty years after their parents passed. When the older brother died, the younger brother refused to show up at the memorial for him.

Fireworks between siblings can become explosive — brothers and sisters and cousins and uncles all begin calling each other the kind of names reserved for barnyard animals and residents of the House of Commons during Question Period.

What's the cause of all this nasty animosity?

It's almost always rooted in the Last Will and Testament that their parents signed or forgot to sign; in other words, money and material things.

If matters become serious enough, each side may hire a lawyer. Lawyers in legal tussles over wills tend to get along wonderfully. The air may be blue above the heads of feuding family members who wanted Mother's cameo broach or Father's oil painting of *Sunset over Sudbury*, but the air in the lawyers' offices is positively pink with delight. Let 'em fight, the hired legal help will say — the clock keeps ticking for us.

Sometimes the greed and anger between family members grows so deep and hostile that the feud continues for years. You may have heard, for example, of the Pritzker family, who operated the Hyatt hotel chain and a bunch of other money-making enterprises for many years. As of 2015, the eleven surviving members of the family had a total net worth of $27 billion, give or take a few hundred million.

Hey, are they rich and happy? No. Most are rich and miserable, which is not a goal anyone should strive for. The family has been battling over their respective inheritances since the death of Jay Pritzker in 2000. He made billions for the family through his life, and no doubt expected to leave the members wealthy, healthy and happy. Somehow he blew it. Only the lawyers are rich and happy.

Think of the irony of this situation, especially for people like you and me whose personal wealth would not form a bubble on the Prizkers' tub of dough.

You build one of the world's great reservoirs of wealth, pass it on to your offspring, and they dedicate their lives to acting like a flock of chickens chasing the last bug in the barnyard.

To avoid this kind of family disaster, you need to do lots of thinking and planning. Your legacy should not be buried in bile; it should be afloat in wisdom and love or as much of both as you can afford to buy from a good lawyer.

For all the advice I'm offering you below, your most important goal should be to avoid confrontation among family members when you are no longer around to tell them to shut up and be nice or some similar admonishment.

One more point before we get started: If you have never arranged an estate plan, consider getting assistance from someone who has seen how other peoples' estate plans were designed and worked. Ask for a reference to a reasonably priced and trusted lawyer and/or estate planner. Then buy a little advice.

So you pay a few bucks for it. Look at it this way: It's not coming out of your pocket. It's coming out of the inheritance of the people you are trying to treat fairly. And who can argue with that?

Where There's a Will…

Have you ever had a guest stay over at your house for a few days — maybe a family member or a good friend from your school days? They stay in your spare room, you all have a good time, they pack to leave, you wave them goodbye — then you go into the room where they were staying, and it's a mess. You spend a lot of time cleaning up, washing this and scrubbing that, doing things that they should have done before they left. But they didn't think about it. They left it for you to handle. Which is selfish, right?

You still have pleasant memories of their visit, but they're not quite as warm as they should have been. "Couldn't they tidy up after themselves?" you might grumble.[6]

Similar things can happen after we all depart this guesthouse called Earth. Except it has little to do with dirty laundry and lots to do with other stuff we accumulated through our lives. Which might still include dirty laundry, but forget it for now…

The answer is to plan your departure. This way, you won't leave a mess for your family and maybe your friends to clean up after you.

It's easy to say, "Like I should care?" Yes, you should.

Among other things, having a well-constructed will can put more of the things you accumulated through your life into the

---

6   Actually, this tends to be the response of women more than men, wives more than husbands, but you get the point I'm sure.

hands of the people you care about instead of into the hands of the government. Unless you have warmer feelings for the government than you have for your own family, this makes it a good move.

Taking Stock

I suggest you take a rainy Sunday — or a sunny Monday, it doesn't matter — and sit down with a pencil and paper, or an iPad, or a computer and make an inventory of your assets and liabilities. It's an important part of making sure you don't leave a mess behind when you go.

Start by writing down the date of the list, then record all of your assets. Include these items, if you have them:

ASSETS

- Your home and vacation property.

- Investments you own, both registered (as in an RRSP, RRIF, or TFSA) and unregistered.

- All of your bank accounts — where they are and the account numbers.

- Insurance policies and annuities, including their face value.

- Personal stuff — cars, boats, jewellery, artwork.

- Pension assets, if you contributed to a company pension plan, while working.

- The current value of any businesses you may own or have an interest in, like your brother-in-law's dry cleaning store or your own donut shop.

Now list the money you owe and to whom you owe it as of the date at the top of the page of your list.

LIABILITIES

- A mortgage on your home or vacation property.

- Investment-related debt — money you own in stocks you may have purchased as an investment.

- Credit card debts.

- Money owed on things you may have bought on some kind of payment plan — car, furniture, boat.

- Personal obligations, including family support payments.

Start a new list. This one doesn't itemize what you own, or what you owe. It tells everyone where this list is, along with other important documents. It might be wise to put at least some of the stuff shown below in a safe-deposit box or a lockable, fire-resistant metal container. This stash should include:

- A will and a power of attorney, which dictates who can take over running things if you're incapacitated due to an accident or illness. If you have neither of these, call a good lawyer as soon as you finish following all the suggestions in this chapter and have them prepared for you.

- Your birth and marriage certificates.

- Marriage contracts, including prenuptial agreements.

- Insurance policies.

- Deeds to your home, vacation property, or any other real estate you own.

- The location of the safe deposit box (or some other place) where you are putting all of these goodies.

- Details of any pre-planned funeral arrangements you may have made.

- The names and addresses of your professional advisors, including lawyer, accountant, financial consultant, stockbroker, and so on.

Keep this list handy and tell someone you trust about it and where to find it.

Now it's time to make some hard decisions. Actually, they may be easy for you, if you know exactly who you want to benefit from the treasure you built up over your life. You may want to give this a lot of thought before putting pen to paper. Or finger to iPad. Or hands to computer keyboard. Whatever.

The legal term is "Transfer of Assets". That means you're passing on the stuff you accumulated over your lifetime to people you feel deserve it — things like money, houses, land, furniture, jewellery, and so on. There are five ways to do it. Most of us need only one, but it's worth knowing the choices.

1. *Gifting Assets.* This is easy. You choose the things you want to pass on, before you do the same, and hand them out as gifts. If you choose to hand them to a licensed charity, you can even earn some tax benefits.

2. *Testamentary Trusts.* Don't let the name scare you. It just means that, as part of your will, you arrange to transfer ownership of assets to somebody, under the terms of the trust. (Lawyers love this kind of stuff.)

3. *Living Trust.* This is like a Testamentary Trust, but it happens while you are still alive to witness it.

4. *Joint Ownership.* Since we're talking about transferring assets from you to someone else, this is an easy way to do it. Lawyers call the usual version *Joint Tenancy with Right of Survivorship.* When one person dies, ownership automatically transfers to the surviving person. Very neat, but it may involve some tax and other legal concerns.

5. *Wills.* Everyone should have one. Really. The primary purpose of a will is to describe how you want to transfer your assets when you are gone. This sounds easy, right?

Sometimes it is, sometimes it's not. Before you list who gets what (and maybe why) in your will, invest some time in thinking about things carefully. Look at it this way: You spent a lifetime gathering what you want to pass on; doesn't it make sense to spend a few minutes deciding how to dispose of it on the safe assumption that you won't be needing any of it at some point?

You should also draft a *Living Will*, sometimes called a Power of Attorney for Personal Care or an Advance Healthcare Directive. Some people find this part of planning at this stage of their life difficult to handle because it deals with things like strokes, communications issues related to incapacity, and a lot of other things that happen to people your age but you hope will never happen to you.

They may happen to you anyway, and if/when they do, somebody is going to have to make some hard decisions. Why let other people make them — or even *force* them to make them — when you can do it now, while you are still hale and hearty and sharp as a tack?

Simply put, a Living Will includes instructions on what is to be done about medical care if you are so disabled that you are unable to tell people what you want done. At its sharpest edge, it deals with things you do *not* want done, such as extreme attempts to revive you if your condition is essentially hopeless or if revival means your quality of life will be similar to that of a tree stump. (Doesn't hurt to have a little humour now and then when discussing these things.)

Without legally binding instructions on how to deal with these questions, your family would need the courts to consider and make a decision, which involves spending money and assuming that the court's decision is the same one you would have chosen if you were able to do so.

You can hand this power to anybody you choose — an adult child, your spouse, a close friend, or a trust officer. You can name two people if you want and say whether you prefer that they work together (jointly) or separately. You should, of course, tell the lucky nominees of your choice.

That's the easy part. The hard part is taking time to think about it seriously, then having the papers drawn up.

Your Estate

Making out your will and similar documents is not something you should do over a cup of coffee. This is serious stuff, and you and your family should take the process equally seriously.

Start by asking yourself the questions below and write down the appropriate answers for your own reference. Incidentally, "estate" does not necessarily mean a ranch in Alberta or Downton Abbey. It can mean your suburban house, your rusty minivan, and the insurance policy you bought over the phone one weekend. They are your assets, and it's up to you to decide who gets them when you're gone. Don't leave it up to anyone else to decide. That's unfair.

- *Who will be the beneficiaries of your estate?* You might ask for help from a lawyer on this one. Your surviving spouse, your children, your favourite relative, a good friend, a charitable cause — they may all benefit (thus "beneficiaries") from your decision, but you need to give it some thought.

- *What kind of impact do you want your estate plan to have on your family?* Do you want them to receive cold hard cash to use as they see fit? If you have a business, are you hoping they will choose to operate it? Think of the most important assets on that list you made earlier. Now imagine them in the hands of the various people you may choose. What will they do with them? What do you *want* them to do with them?

This is especially important if you own a business that you want to stay operating after you're gone. A major mistake made by some people in this situation is to assume that their family members share the same dream as them. Surprise — they may not. If that's the case, deal with it ahead of time. Sell the business, set aside the earnings from it, and leave the cash instead of the corporation.

A Cautionary Tale

I know of a man who launched a successful electronics distributing company when his children were young. He remained the sole owner of the operation, which included a large warehousing and office building in north Toronto.

The man had two sons, born about five years apart. The eldest son rose through the company from salesman to manager, all the way to CEO, and he was ready to take over the corporation when his father passed on. The youngest son worked in the warehouse now and then, when he wasn't managing local rock bands with generally little success.

The father was proud of both sons, although somewhat nearsighted about their virtues and drawbacks. The eldest son resented his younger brother's "artsy" approach to life, and the younger son lacked both a knack and an interest in business if it didn't include guitars, drums and groupies.

On his own, the father came up with this solution: The elder son would inherit the corporation with all of its growth opportunities and complications, and the younger son would receive the building and the land it sat on. The corporation would pay $10,000 monthly rent to the younger son and be responsible for all maintenance costs on the property. Was this, as some people in America like to say when describing their view of the world, fair and balanced?

No, it was not.

The younger son was ecstatic. Ten grand a month would be deposited in his account for the rest of his life, with annual increases tied to the cost of living. It was like winning a lottery.

The older son was…well, *not* ecstatic. Through all the ups and downs of the business, he would have to deposit $10,000 or more in his brother's bank account each month no matter what his profit-and-loss statement said. True, he stood to earn much more than his younger sibling each year, but only if he continued to work hard at operating the firm and avoided many pitfalls that his kind of business encountered.

The older brother seethed, he grumbled, he refused to have anything to do with his kid brother, and he paid large legal fees to have the situation changed by the courts without success.

He also lost a good deal of drive to maintain the business against strong competition. When the business began to fail, the older brother decided to get out from under the responsibility. He sold the company at a price lower than its book cost. The new owner successfully broke the lease and moved the business to a new location, leaving the younger son with an empty building, which he sold at a bargain price.

Some people familiar with the company blamed changing market conditions for the company's problems. Others said it was poor management. A few suggested that the older brother let things slide out of spite toward his younger brother, but nobody can take that kind of action just because he's angry with his brother, right?

Yes, they can. And do.

Here's a fact to remember: Very few family businesses survive past the third generation. The biggest reason: Poor planning to deal with the retirement, disability, or the passing of the owner.

If you sincerely want your business to continue as a going concern after you're gone, invest a lot of thought and planning into it. You might consider, for example, a buy-sell plan backed by a life insurance policy that can transfer the business to whomever you choose at a fair market value. There are other alternatives, and once again it's worth investing a few bucks and a little time to see that things are done right.

Give some thought — wait — give a LOT of thought to naming the Executor of your estate.

Being named the Executor of the estate of a friend or close relative sounds like a big deal. And it is — big enough that you should think long and hard about who you name, even if your estate is modest in size.

Acting as an Executor is not an empty honour. You shouldn't say, "Suzie (or Seth or whoever), you've been a good friend to me all these years, so here's what I want to do for you: I am naming you the Executor of my estate. Doesn't that make you feel great?"

If Suzie or Seth know what's involved in being an Executor, they may not be prepared to give you a hug and buy you a drink. They may say, "Gee, thanks — you shouldn't have", and really mean it. Because being an executor of an estate is not always an honour. It can be lot of hard work.

Here are some things expected of an Executor:

1. *Disburse property* to the beneficiaries, according to the instructions in your will.

2. *Obtain information* on potential heirs.

3. *Collect and arrange payment* of the estate's debts.

4. *Confirm, deny, approve or disapprove* creditor claims.

5. *Make sure estate taxes are calculated,* forms are filed, and tax payments are made.

6. *Assist the attorney* in handling concerns of the estate.

7. *Act as a legal conveyor* to designate where donations will be sent according to instructions in the will.

8. *Represent the estate* with the ability to sue or be sued on behalf of the estate.

9. *Hold legal title* to the estate property (but the Executor cannot use the title or property for his/her own benefit, unless permitted by the terms of the will).

10. *Serve as the target* for various disagreements, complaints, protests, objections, and general grumbling of beneficiaries or wannabe beneficiaries who feel they have been cheated, overlooked, and generally bamboozled.

That's What Friends Are For

Duty number ten is not listed in the general legal guide to all the things executors must do, but it's a common development anyway, usually based on the previous nine things Executors are expected to look after.

As you can see, this is not the kind of chore you should assign to someone who believes they can carry it out between periods of a hockey game. You need someone who can make decisions, agrees to take the job seriously, and respects both you and your wishes. Oh, and they should have one more quality: Money.

How can money help a wealthy (relatively speaking) Executor do a better job? By making it less likely that they will make decisions that benefit themselves over the beneficiaries. It's also because there is no legal provision for an Executor to be reimbursed for all the work they do in carrying out your instructions, something to keep in mind when naming the best person you know to do things you want done.

Some questions worth considering:

- *If you own a thriving business, why not have two wills?* One would deal with your personal assets, and the other would help dispose of your business. Again, a good estate planner can handle this. Find one, consider their advice, take it if you agree and don't resent paying their fees. Remember whose pocket it is coming from eventually.

- *When do you want your beneficiaries to receive their inheritance?* Immediately? When they reach a certain age? Turning a large amount of cash over to people still in their teens — or just out of them — can be a risky venture. Should they wait until they are 21 or older?

- *What about charities? Who would you like to benefit from your estate, and how much should they receive?* This is becoming popular, I hear. I'm not sure why. Are people becoming more generous? Are our offspring doing well enough on their own? Do we not trust our family members to spend the money wisely?

Spare the Heirs

One more thing to worry about so that your beloved heirs won't have to: How do you want your funeral handled?

Even if you don't want a formal service, you need to let people know what to do when you're gone. And where to do it. And how. By the way, it would be good if you pay for it yourself. In advance. This is no time to be stingy.

Planning and preparing for things after your passing isn't really about the money. It's about the literally last kind thing you can do for your family, the last way you can express your love for them in a kind of off-handed way.

Here's why: Assuming you have led your life in a way that earned you at least some level of respect and affection from those around you, they're going to miss you when you're gone. It will be a stressful time for them. They need to mourn and grieve your passing. What they *don't* need is the pressure of making tough decisions and tracking down various odds and ends without you to guide them.

It may be difficult for some people to deal with this kind of stuff, but if you refuse to tackle it ahead of time — if you leave family members guessing about what should be done at a difficult time for all of them — that's selfish.

I'm not exaggerating. In case you haven't been asked to carry out the duties of making funeral arrangements and handling other chores for someone who left everything up to others, here are just some of the things involved:

- Gathering all the data needed to make things official, including locating birth certificate, citizenship details, etc.

- Choosing the funeral home, pallbearers, cemetery, flowers or arranging donations from friends and relatives, music and speakers at the funeral service (if there is one), and taking similar steps if the choice is cremation — not to mention, deciding who makes this choice.

- Spreading the word among family and friends and in newspaper announcements, including writing all the words in the death notice, and hoping no one gets angry because they were not included or if things were in the wrong order or...you get the idea.

- Performing chores that the executor of your Will (You will have a Will, won't you?) is not expected to do, such as dealing with insurance agents, financial planners, credit cards, banks, lawyers and other people many of us tend to avoid.

- Paying for all the expenses associated with the above.

Plan Your Own Send-Off

Remember — all of those decisions need to be done within a few days by people who you can assume are already shaken by your passing.

By pre-arranging your funeral, you can spare them from the financial and emotional burden that comes at a difficult time.

It doesn't have to be expensive. You can choose the Rolls-Royce option with gold casket, choir, and Cadillacs, if you like. Or you can choose a simple gathering followed by sandwiches and coffee. It's your money and your life.

There's a double benefit to handling things this way: First, you will know that things will be done the way you want them to be done, as opposed to somebody else's idea of what should be done.

And second, your last act will be one of the most loving and caring things you can do for your family. It will leave them thinking, "Wasn't he/she a great guy/gal?"

FIFTEEN

Hello, I Must Be Going

Through much of our lives, we all tell ourselves the same lie, and the lie is this: *I'm going to live forever!*

I told myself the same thing.

And hey — so far, so good.

Through our 30s, 40s, and 50s, we go through life assuming that our mortality is nothing but a rumour. Sometime in our 60s, when our remaining hair is grey and parts of our body could use an overhaul, we realize that eventually the world will have to get along without us. And that day could be sooner than we think.

So what should we do about it?

Three things: First, we should remind ourselves of a basic law of marketing that says lowering the supply of a commodity while increasing the demand escalates its value. It works with oil, with salt and, believe it or not, with life.

The days remaining in your life are a finite commodity; they always were, of course, but now that you can almost count them, you appreciate their increased value. Meanwhile, you start demanding more out of life because you recognize all the things you've yet to do that you promised yourself to do. So every day is more precious than the last. That makes it more important to enjoy them and not squander them.

Next, as I detailed in the preceding chapter, we should pay attention to those who will be around after we're gone. The days following your passing will mean nothing to you, but they will be important to those you care about. You can make them easier by investing in life insurance that will help your family through the time without you and by making arrangements and prepaying for the things you want done. It's difficult to think about what these decisions involve, but it will be even more difficult on others if you don't deal with them now.

Finally, give some thought to the legacy you'll leave. And not the kind you're probably thinking about.

If you tie your identity entirely to the wealth you've accumulated during your working years, enjoy all your money while you can, but don't expect the size of your bank account to define you in the minds of other people. Sure, they might be impressed by the fact that you pulled yourself out of poverty without robbing a bank. But whenever I hear praise for people at their funeral or memorial service, the admiration is never connected to the money they left behind; it's about the way they lived their lives on a personal level.

"She was always there to help others," is one example. Some others are: "He was a real gentleman, the warmest, sweetest man you could imagine," and "She was loved and admired by so many people." It's true that now and then I've heard less flattering comments whispered among mourners who wished they were elsewhere. I have never heard, however, praise based on lines such as "He made himself a billion dollars" or "She had a trunk-load of diamonds". It just doesn't matter anymore to other people. And for sure, it won't matter to you either.

You will be remembered most, not for what you earned, but for who you were as a person, as a friend, as a parent, and as a human being. That's the legacy worth building, and it's one that we can all leave behind us regardless of how much money we made, how much property we owned, and how many toys we accumulated.

Lucky Man

I have heard somebody at a funeral service suggest that a successful man or woman had been "lucky" in his or her life, as though this was an admirable quality. Comments like that make me uncomfortable because I have a real problem identifying how much luck played a part in my life. The good kind, I mean.

To be honest, I don't think it did. Not in a big way.

Earlier, I mentioned how lucky I was to have Rhoda as my life partner. I could brag a little, I suppose, and say that I chose her all those years ago because I recognized her great qualities even when we were both teenagers. "It wasn't luck," I could say. "I just happened to be smart enough to choose her and forget about all the others."

I suspect that some people look at me, the company that Rhoda and I built, our family of great kids who make us proud every day, and the financial security we've accumulated — and they say something like, "Boy, were they lucky!"

Lucky? What was so lucky about me working the midnight shift in my first Canadian winter, schlepping luggage onto Air Canada planes for people to fly south to Florida or Jamaica? Or deciding to start a capital-intensive business renting cars when the banks were charging 22 percent annual interest?

I don't resent having to do those things, and I sure don't regret them. They had to be done at the time, and I was glad to have the chance to do them. I'll admit that, over the years, Rhoda and I escaped some of the tragedies of various kinds that can befall families. I suppose that can be described as being lucky.

But if we were lucky in business, it was never something we counted on. And I advise you not to count on luck to carry you through life with maximum pleasure and minimum pain. Instead of luck, count on yourself. Count on your hard work, your determination to succeed, your vision, and from time to time your family and friends.

Just don't count on being lucky.

I know you've probably heard this line before, but here it is from me: *The harder I worked, the luckier I got.*

By the way, if you choose to start your own business, and carve out your own success with hard work and dedication: Good luck.

The Last Word

Now that I'm (mostly) retired, I've had time to think about stuff that I couldn't, or refused to, think about in the past. This is probably the best place to share it.

As I write this I'm looking forward to another ten or fifteen good years. Maybe more, maybe less, but this is a realistic figure. By good I mean good health and mobility to do most of the things I want to do where and when I want to do them. I have asked myself, "Herb, what do you need to get through those years with as much pleasure and satisfaction as possible?" They are, as I mentioned above, valuable years after all, and I don't want to waste a minute of them.

I boiled things down to Five Fs to pass on to you now. A couple may surprise you, but it's fun to have a surprise now and then, right? Here they are:

Herb's Five Fs to Value Late in Life

1. FAITH. This one may be a surprise because I've never been much of a fan of religion. But this book isn't just about me; it's about other people who may have a different view of spiritual things. A lot of them get hope, courage, and inspiration from their faith, and if this includes you, then hold onto and treasure it. Me, I'm for whatever helps get you through the night…

2. FAMILY. I'm including everyone close to you who loves you in the broadest sense of the term — your family along with your closest friends, who are often just like

family to you. Never take any of them for granted — they are among your most treasured assets.

3. FITNESS. Take care of yourself. Watch your diet, get regular check-ups, avoid smoking and too much drinking, and generally use your head to look after your body.

    This can be a challenge if you have lived your life until now with all the care and attention that I pay to my old pair of slippers. All that neglect and harsh treatment catches up on us eventually. By the time we're in our 60s, we're more wear-and-tear than heart-and-soul.

    It's still not too late to end bad habits and start good ones. You already know the sermon: Avoid tobacco, drugs, and excessive alcohol. Get a regular check-up and listen to your doctor's advice. (Note to men: And listen to your spouses too. This will not only likely improve your health, but also smooth things at home.) Look for ways to move around, such as taking long walks or doing some gardening chores. You may not improve your body to Hollywood Super Star status, but if you can maintain its current state for an extra few years, you're a winner.

4. FORTUNE. You don't need to be rich, and you shouldn't be stingy. Build up the funds you need and manage them yourself with help from a trusted advisor. Then be prepared to share them with others. Ask anybody in their 60s or 70s what they would do if they won a major lottery — say, 30 or 40 million dollars. Almost all of them will give you the same answer: "I would give all or most of it away." There's a lesson in that.

5. FREEDOM. With planning and luck, you'll have more of it in your retirement than you ever had in your working years. Use it to seek adventure, have fun, and celebrate the joy of being alive in a world that is not as

bad as it appears some days and often can be better than you expect.

So What?

I suspect I'm somewhere ahead of you in my life journey, which means I've seen more of the road. If so, I'm advising you to look ahead in your own life, all the way up to where I am in mine. When you get there, try to visualize the things I've described in this book — like seeing the end of the trip somewhere down the highway ahead of us, you and me.

You may not believe it, but the end of the highway is not leaving. You are. Sometime. This shouldn't be a source of fear or sadness. Think of it as motivation to recognize some of the things I've listed above and deal with them — things like making a will and having serious discussions with family.

Because, one way or another, you'll need to. You can do it now. Or you can do it later. I think now is better.

I haven't acquired all the knowledge I need or want over my life so far, but I've spent the last forty thousand words sharing many of these thoughts and ideas with you. It's up to you to remember or forget them, accept them or reject them, use them or lose them.

If one piece of my wisdom stays with you, I hope it's this:

The journey that I've mentioned throughout this book is travelled on one-way roads.

You can choose the route, but you can't change the destination.

You can set your pace, but you can't change the speed.

You can admire the scenery, but you won't know when the trip ends.

You can hold the wheel, but you're not always in control.

The best thing to do is plan your journey in such a way that you get as much out of the trip as possible. While you're at it, prepare yourself for unexpected events I referred to earlier, the kind that can happen on any trip — detours, potholes, hitch-hikers, and some jerk in the next car giving you the finger.

It's your life and your journey. Enjoy it in as much comfort with as many friends as you can gather around you.

I'd suggest that you travel in a car rented from Discount, but Rhoda might think I'm going too far.

Bon Voyage.

Au Revoir.

Auf Wiedersehen.

Despedida.

Adieu.

Adios.

Shalom.

THE END

Printed in Canada